GETHSEMANE

to

GALILEE

Bible Talks of The New Testament
by Master Teacher

ENDEAVOR ACADEMY
Certum Est Quia Impossibile Est

International Standard Book Number (ISBN-10)1-890648-11-6

(ISBN-13) 978-1-890648-11-4

Published By:
Endeavor Academy
501 East Adams Street
Wisconsin Dells, WI 53965, U. S. A.
Tel: +1 (608) 254-4431 Fax: +1 (608) 253-2892
Website: www.themasterteacher.tv

Email: publishing@endeavoracademy.com

Contents

What I tell you in darkness,
that speak ye in light:
and what ye hear in the ear,
that preach ye upon the housetops.

Preface

The entire teachings and demonstrations of Jesus Christ are immediate, direct, sustained confrontations between the inevitability of a whole, perfectly-loving, eternally-creating God, compared to the isolation, pain and sickness, loss and death of this place called Earth. To attempt to connect the divinely-revealing declarations of Jesus Christ, even in regard to the very fundamental question "what is life," to the so-called Christian Institution, or indeed any worldly establishment, is totally unreasonable and absurdly impossible. You will search in vain in the New Testament among the direct utterances of Jesus, except for an occasional placation of the Pharisees, for any quotations in His fundamental philosophy of spiritual reality that will be unqualifyingly acceptable to institutional or governing authorities or to any constituencies called human society.

The imperative of direct, individual, personal experience of the revelation of God is the only fundamental necessity of His entire teaching. There is absolutely no allowance for the worldly condition of separation from an eternally-creating God. In order for the divine message of Jesus Christ to have any reasonable meaning, its uncompromising unconditionality must be accepted, admitted and asserted. In other words, He must be allowed to mean exactly what He says. What could possibly merit crucifixion more than the seditious instruction that you "love your enemies" (Matthew 5:44) and "resist not evil" (Matthew 5:39)?

Subversive elements that seriously propagate the tenets that "you don't belong in this world" (John 15:19) and demand that you admit that you are "perfect, even as your Father in Heaven is perfect" (Matthew 5:48) **must** be denied, attacked and finally destroyed.

You may be happily surprised to discover the light of an exciting, whole new understanding of New Testament scripture, if you will let the premises of your discernment be based on three simple postulations that Jesus teaches:

-There is one wholly-loving, eternally-creating God, who creates you and everything in the universe perfectly.

-Though you appear separate from this creative Love, you may at any moment, using the power of your mind, return to Heaven through the transformation of this apparent physical and mental condition of loss of reality – to the memory that you are still always and only at home in Heaven.

-In New Testament scripture, He is instructing you very specifically in the manner in which this is done. Our Savior, Jesus Christ, teaches the simple catechism of unconditional love, certainty of eternal life gained by revelation, and resurrection through continuing uncompromising, unconditional surrender to the eternal, perfectly-creating Will of God.

M. T.

And if I go and prepare a place for you,
I will come again, and receive you unto myself;
that where I am, there ye may be also.
And whither I go ye know, and the way ye know.

A new commandment I give unto you,
That ye love one another;
as I have loved you,
that ye also love one another.

1 Corinthians 13

It's an incredible occurrence for me to hear the words of Jesus Christ, first hand scripture of *A Course In Miracles*, read in a denominational setting – that is, a coming together of free Christians, expressing the literal word of our Master Jesus Christ. It's impossible to follow that. What you have done within the framework of the fabric of space/time, historic occurrence, is the taking of the great teacher, awakened man, Jesus Christ of Nazareth, at His word of 2000 years ago, and for the very first time bringing it to a holy place, gathering together in an association of the progression of transforming mind, the secret, incredible, mystical teachings of Christianity.

The simple statement that natural man, as he is constituted in his perceptual mis-evaluations can, through a process of relinquishment of those perceptual observations come to know his true heritage as the Living Son of God. That's what's happening here. And that's incredible. To listen to your willingness to confess your perfection in a land where the establishment of religion is based on the confession of sin is an extraordinary thing. To see a gathering of human beings willing to base their determination to find God on their acknowledgment that they are the single Son of God rather than deep sinners who must make irreversible atonement for a guilt that has cast them into hell is an extraordinary thing. It is the fundamental teaching of Jesus Christ of Nazareth.

The connection of The Free Christian Church of Full Purpose to the original, historic church teachings of the disciples or of the apostles may not be completely apparent to you for this reason, and our lovely brother teacher Paul puts it very succinctly when he says that natural man does not know of spiritual man, spiritual man does not know of natural man (I Corinthians 2:14). Our divine brother, the persecutor of Christ, Saul of Tarsus, which you have been, underwent the Damascus experience that made him Paul. You, as modern-day crucifiers of Christ are undergoing your Damascus experience, the transformation of your mind, through the commandment "why do you persecute me" (Acts 9:4) as indicated in the Course to the certainty of the teachings of Jesus Christ. The parallels of Paul in the New Testament will be extraordinary if you are willing to subtract natural man's assertion of the naturalness of Paul and declare through the Course the spiritualness of Paul as you do with your brother and as your teaching directs you. The naturalness of man means nothing. The divinity of man in your declaration means everything. Does that mean that we pick and choose in scripture? Of course. The idea of pick and choose is the necessity to discern spiritual man from natural man. We would not, as new Christians, have a tendency to give a lot of accord to the publishers or scribes of *A Course In Miracles*, would we? We would not naturally do that. From a divine standpoint, the method by which natural man comes to know God is meaningless. It has no meaning. Our emphasis is not then on the idea that natural man, through his own endeavor, can come to know God, but rather by his full commitment to the certainty that he cannot know, he can become Godly.

Paul went through his transformation process and he ended up apparently formulating a natural church that has lasted for 2000 years, and let's give it the full value that it needs, and look at the spiritual nature of today's Christianity rather than the derogatory natural way. If we do that, we will discern through our awakening minds the broad range of allegory and parable that occur in the scriptures. A beautiful demonstration of that, and I know that for many Christians it's cliché, is Paul's Corinthians 13, wherein he defines love. And I'm going to read it to you from an association with the new scripture of Jesus in *A Course In Miracles*. We note first that in the translation from the Greek in the King James Version that love is translated as *charity*. The closest that the expression that Paul meant when he said *love* in the Greek translated to *charity* or *giving*. Love, then, in truth, is nothing but full giving, or full forgiving. Charity, the acknowledgment of the need to serve and help, when it reaches its ultimate point, is the total giving of yourself. In that sense, in the King James translation, *charity* literally means God or God in action or creating. The closest that the perceptual mind can get to creating is giving. This occurs in Corinthians 13, and I'll read it for you. This is a statement by a consciousness who is struggling to express what he feels in his heart, and he acknowledges that he carries a burden of self deep within him. This is an initiate, who having undergone the process, will say very mystical things like: I know a man who went to third heaven, what he saw there I may not disclose. (II Cor 12:2-4) All of the lovely mystical things that occur that have been taken by exoteric or perceptual Christianity and turned into some sort of doctrinal or denominational observation. We, then, as new Christians, proclaim that the sole purpose of the formulation of the establishment of the church is to bring about the transformation of the mind and we gather together with a declaration that through our mutual forgiveness we may see the face of Christ in each other and therein the glory of God shining on us. This is the Church of Jesus Christ.

Paul speaks for himself, and he speaks particularly for the magic of phenomena that can occur in the Simon Magus, the magician, in the awakening process where you discover through the energies the use of wholeness, that you have evolved particular characteristics that transcend normal human purposes, don't they. He directs himself to this with the declaration that unless you are giving wholly of yourself, all of the phenomena that you perform will be totally meaningless. This is I Corinthians 13: Though I speak with the tongues of men and of angels, and have not charity, I am become as sounding brass or a tinkling cymbal. (I Cor 13:1) You notice that he includes the tongues of angels as interpreted by man. Notice that he says that it may sound very beautiful, but where in it is the self aggrandizement, where is there in it the determination to hold on to the expression of the limited self in association with these words?

And though I have the gift of prophecy, and understand all mysteries, and all knowledge; and though I have all faith, so that I could remove mountains, and have not charity, I am nothing. (I Cor 13:2) If I am not able to give wholly of myself. Notice that he says: understand all mysteries. The necessity to understand mysteries is the nature of man, not of God. There is no mystery about God. Understanding mysteries is of man. And have all knowledge... All knowledge on earth falls short of truth. And though I have all faith... That's a declaration or a taking credit for my ability to acknowledge God... so that I could remove mountains... This is the notation that is both in the Course and in the temptations of God, being given the power to act within human resources rather than acknowledging that you are under no laws but God's. Have I not love, I am nothing... Notice that it doesn't say *I have nothing*, what does it say? **I AM NOTHING.** This is the closest that Paul could come to expressing that unless you are love you are nothing. They distort the translations later on because they want it to fit in, but the King James translation had a tendency to take the literal meaning and leave it even though it didn't make any sense. The sense to *I am nothing* has to be looked at from where we're looking at it, in the indication that natural man, or earth, is literally nothing.

And though I bestow all of my goods to feed the poor, and though I give my body to be burned, and have not charity, it profiteth me nothing. (I Cor 13:3) This is the same idea as taking credit for service. This is the same idea as acknowledging that there is something outside of you that is poor that by giving of a limited association of self I can serve God. Charity, or the indication of total service, would be that I give myself totally to the poor. Charity, as defined in the human relationship, or the notation of reciprocity, or the sharing of limitation, of scarcity, of death, is not what love is.

Charity suffereth long, and is kind. (I Cor 13:4) This is the idea that as a true servant of God you will be confronted with the necessity to evolve patience. Blessed are those who are ridiculed in my name. (Mat. 5:11) Charity suffereth long and is kind; charity envieth not. (I Cor 13:4) This is the idea that in our love of God we are not in competition with each other. We are not trying to determine who, through their individual process, is closer to this divine truth than any of our other brothers. There is no envy in us, and there is none in God or in love.

Charity vaunteth not itself... (I Cor 13:4) It doesn't take on credentials. It does not identify itself as doctors or long-term teachers of *A Course In*

Miracles or ministers. It does not vaunteth itself. Charity or love needs no identification. It is perfectly what it is in the giving of itself. Charity vaunteth not itself, is not puffed up. (I Cor 13:4) They changed *puffed up* to something else, but there is something very lovely about letting the translation be *puffed up*. If you've ever seen the self-importance that human beings with their credentials like to take in regard to the teachings of the scripture of God or the scripture of IBM Corporation, or whatever scripture, you see the credit they take for it. Love is not puffed up. We'll let that stay as it is.

Doth not behave itself unseemingly... (I Cor 13:5) That is, does not go out and flaunt its nature in association with the prostitution of itself in relationship with the passions with which it is endowed in purity... . seeketh not her own... (I Cor 13:5) Does not indulge in special love. Love does not seeketh her own, love knows her own. This is Paul's attempt to get you away from special relationships. You don't seek your own in the sense that love does not conceive, love creates through the charity... is not easily provoked... (I Cor 13:5) Well, we all get by with that very easily... . and thinketh no evil at all. (I Cor 13:5) *Thinketh no evil* means that love does not know of evil. Evil being death, life being love, life does not know of death. Life is not the opposite of death, it is nothing. Love is not the opposite of evil, which is separation or sin, separation is nothing.

Rejoiceth not in iniquity, but rejoiceth in the truth... (I Cor 13:6) This is what Jesus calls in the Course, the subtle attraction of mutual guilt. Rejoicing not in iniquities means that somewhere underneath you're not happy when your brother is brought down. That's a tough one. This is the nature of your new, evolved man to spiritual man who sees only the uprising of natural man – who as Jesus says sees an attack as a call for help. And that's tough.

Beareth all things, believeth all things, hopeth all things, endureth all things. (I Cor 13:7) Wow! *Believeth all things* – love, charity, has no perception. It believes everything. When I say to you: believe everything! What difference does it make if you love? Once more, the requirement of love, what love is: it *beareth all things* – it steps back, it doesn't confront, it doesn't resist evil... . *believeth all things, hopeth all things...* It's going to happen now. Here comes God, God is coming, the world is over, we're going home. Say AMEN! Wow, it's been a while.

I'll bet it's been a 100 years – we're all old stump preachers. Everybody that comes around this group is a natural carrier of true messages. We may not have always been true with it, but we've always attempted to be true. That's why what you call the Free Christian Church is so missionary. You guys have a lot of memories in you of doing this. You are communicators of love. It's nice to see that this is what Paul was. It's nice to see that the founder of Christianity obviously is Paul, we're aware of that – but these are the divine things that he said that were somehow interpreted into "Goulashes 4" or something... When natural man quotes the scripture, he always finds the natural things. This is how the Course is often taught. You can always give credit to the process if you wish to, rather than seeing that the process doesn't mean anything.

Beareth all things, believeth all things, hopeth all things, endureth all things. Charity never faileth... (I Cor 13:7-8) It has no where to go. If you love, you couldn't possibly fail, you have already failed... . but whether there be prophecies, they shall fail... (I Cor 13:8) This means that the perceptual mind can prophecy its future organization, but will fail simply because the perceptual mind is not capable of a whole prophecy. All prophecies are self-fulfilling unto themselves, but fail because contained within the context of man is a limited goal that he prophecies, and indeed it is fulfilled. We teach prophecy only God now, and it will be fulfilled in its entirety... . whether there be tongues, they shall cease; whether there be knowledge, it shall vanish away. (I Cor 13:8) This is Jesus' lovely statement: beyond time, beyond the stars, beyond the most beautiful things you can imagine in your mind, God is, and that this fails, and God and charity and love does not. Whether there be knowledge, it shall vanish away... and never have been.

For we know in part, and we prophesy in part. (I Cor 13:9) This is the limited association. No matter what it does, since it is partial, it cannot know the truth. But when that which is perfect is come, then that which is in part shall be done away. (I Cor 13:10) Where is the darkness when there is light? Where is the ego, where is the self which was nothing, when the realization of your Godliness comes? It never was. It is not now, as Paul says, and never was.

When I was a child, I spake as a child, I understood as a child, I thought as a child; but when I became a man (a spiritual man) I put away childish things. (I Cor 13:11) So often in the Course Jesus says to you: put away your little childish things. And by that He means your greed, and your envy and your sickness and your death and your self associations. Those are childish things – the idea of sin – too ridiculous for a whole mind to even entertain. And this is what Paul, in his new spiritual mind, is trying to say. He is saying this 2000 years ago, with three separate translations, and it still holds up beautifully. Why? Because he had a true mind, and he was trying to express it. I understood as a child, I thought as a child, but when I became a man, I put away childish things. Now here's the Course: For now we see through a glass, darkly; but then face to face; now I know in part; but then shall I know even as also I am known. (I Cor 13:12)

For now we see through a glass, darkly... that means that we have projected from us an image of ourselves, as image, but it's a partial image, so we can't know totally our association with God... . *but then face to face*. This is the seeing of the face of Christ in your brother... . now I know in part, but then shall I know even as also I am known. The idea of being known totally is the same as knowing totally. This is the practice of *A Course In Miracles*.

And now abideth faith, hope, charity, these three; but the greatest of these is charity. (I Cor 13:13) God bless the reading of these words.

How important perhaps is your connection with the historic teachings of Christianity. Here's a mystical reason: The mystical reason for the necessity of the scripture is that you are the scripture. All of the memories of man, of Christians, in their struggle to teach this, however falsely, for whatever limited purpose, in whatever method of persecution or direction or war or needs to protect and defend; establishments of Vaticans and Constantinoples and churches and holy cities – contained in all of you is the historic beauty of the fundamental certainty of the teachings of Jesus Christ. To throw them away would be absurd. All we would found is a new religion that would say exactly what this says – not what natural man thinks it says, but what we, through our new minds, have come to know that it says, and are taking abroad with us in this endeavor.

To watch the maturing of this new light insight in this time is a momentous and beautiful thing and I want you to understand, if you can, that no matter how momentous you would make it, no matter how much fullness you attempt to give it, you could have no idea of the actual nature in truth of what's really occurring here because perceptual mind is not capable of a total gratitudinal realization – when it is, it is no longer here. That's why we are teaching that truth is coming to truth. But you listen to me, the more now that you acknowledge that this is in fact occurring, and in fact occurred despite the methods in which you attempted to present it, the more quickly will come about the shortening of the time when you will see that this is long ago past away and is no more, and we are gone from here, and we are in the heaven that we never left. Therein lies the peace of God.

Will this now be spread abroad? Will this be heard? Yes. How could it not be? The ceremony that was performed here today is so purely Christian that it is incredible. It's so beautifully an expression of Jesus Christ, who we now realize has always been with us. As we undergo the ordeal, in the admission of our naturalness coming to truth, we see that by the single admission that He has undergone it, we eliminate all the necessity for ourselves to pursue the useless paths where we thought we could find it – this is propitiation at its very highest declaration. Many of you remember being children when you asked the question: why is it if Jesus Christ saved the world we're still here unsaved? The very simple answer is: because you have not acknowledged that He in fact saved the world. If He in fact did, you in fact are not here, and in fact are not. Each moment it only becomes necessary in the method of our certainty to declare that He in fact saved the world, because obviously one saving would be all saving since one sin is all sin. You have in hand these lovely scriptures coming directly from the source that directs you to this. How could you not form a church? You are the church. Our gratitude to you as you emerge now as teachers, as an individual declaration of your transformation. You're going to have the spiritual temerity to go out and read your Confession of Perfection and watch how quickly the Christian who, somewhere in his heart, understood that the New Covenant was only love and did not contain the continuing elements of the necessity to condemn, attack or defend yourself from your brother, will come to meet you and say: yes! I see in you what Jesus taught.

There's a notation that divine makes divine and as your new minds begin to express themselves in the creations of your heart/ mind, in the passion of your own dedication you become true through the relinquishment of the guilt of your apparent falsity by the confession of unqualified determination to get this, so that your peace comes automatically and fully by the simple statement: this is what I'm going to do. This brings you into the now. It subtracts and includes all possibilities, all prophecies become meaningless to you. That's what you're sharing together. That is a free, new church.

Ye are the light of the world.
A city that is set on an hill cannot be hid.
Neither do men light a candle,
and put it under a bushel,
but on a candlestick;
and it giveth light unto all that are in the house.
Let your light so shine before men,
that they may see your good works,
and glorify your Father which is in heaven.

CHAPTER TWO

The Sermon
On The Mount

Good morning free Christians. The magnitude of the happening dawning on us now – it's still a dream, but see how it's changed. See how this coming together now in this association in this temple of worship has brought about a change that's astonishing. Suddenly the word "freedom" doesn't mean free to go out and do things. It doesn't mean free to search yourself; it doesn't mean free to act. It doesn't mean free to have opinions. Freedom now means free to *be*. Free to be what you are through a process taught by a master teacher, by Jesus Christ of Nazareth, beginning 2000 years ago and progressing in the mind of man to this moment. You have learned to relinquish the little man, the past man, the man that is gone away, the man that is no more, and come into the realization that you are in fact as God created you. For the first time in the history of man, as it is constituted in this time framework, you have gathered together to express these words of Jesus Christ that He said just a moment ago. For indeed, in terms of time, this 2000 years since He stood on the mount and made these declarations and you listened down below, and then took your place on the mount and made these declarations are all a part of this association of your perceptual mind that has occurred in this dream that has now become a real dream.

You are free now to be as you are, a freedom brought about by your willingness, as taught so beautifully by Jesus in this new scripture, *A Course in Miracles,* to relinquish what you thought you were. Give up the past in the certainty that atonement is with you as you free yourself from your own limited perceptions. That's what a free Christian is. And that is what you are. As you begin now to act and speak in spirit, not in the perceptual declaration of yourself, but through the release of your perceptual declarations, speaking directly from the whole truth of you as the Christ. This is what you are becoming.

To bring this together for you – the teachings of the Course and the teachings of the New Testament – I'm going to do a little from Matthew, chapters 5, 6 and 7 which is *A Course In Miracles* – the Sermon on the Mount – so that you can see that the teachings of Jesus as He presents them to you are exactly the same teachings He presented to you seven days ago, a hundred years ago, a thousand years ago – when as an awakening man He stood on the mount and addressed you. The astonishing thing about this is this has survived, spoken in Aramaic, spoken in a strange language not even written in any regard for 30 years, then processed through Greek to the Latin and surviving in monasteries for hundreds of years being reorganized, brought up to a translation in the 1600s into English, being revised again and again. And still, as I take this now and read it to you, your new minds will make a connection to show you that He's standing on the mount now, doing the same thing. The whole teaching is that time itself is not sequential. With your new free minds, you can picture yourself as I read these words, to the direction of what's been occurring here. What we say here and practice here is what He will admonish you to do in the Sermon on the Mount.

This is the Holy Bible from the Gideons, the King James version, but you can't take the truth out of it because the truth of Jesus is what He says. Down through the ages they've attempted to subtract the man from the message, which is exactly what they try to do today with *A Course In Miracles.* But what Jesus Christ of Nazareth says here is what He says in *A Course In Miracles.* You have come to know with your new whole mind that what He says is what He is. If you no longer retain these perceptions of your limited self, what you say is what you are going to be.

When He goes up onto the mount, it's interesting that the translation goes: And seeing the multitudes, he went up into a mountain: and when he was set, his disciples came to Him. He was prepared for them, He went ahead of them. And he opened his mouth, and taught them, saying. (Matthew 5:1-2) Notice that it doesn't say that He suddenly began to speak. It says: *he opened his mouth* and then He spoke. What He said was not coming from his associations with his mouth, was it? No. He opened his mouth, and then He spoke in the spirit of his reality. He said the things that you look at in the translations that they haven't been able to change. Isn't that nice to see? They will remain that way. I'm going to pick it up in Matthew 6:19.

Lay not up for yourself treasures upon earth, where moth and rust doth corrupt, and where thieves break through and steal... This is a declaration that perceptual mind in scarcity, which is what you are, will lose in three ways: The moths will eat it. That means it will be consumed by you (these are thought forms now) or by somebody else. If you try to hold onto it and not use it, what will happen? It will rust and tarnish. Or, if you don't guard it sufficiently, what will happen? Thieves will break in and take it away. Do you see? Those are the three things you protect in your own perceptual mind. You try to preserve it, but it rots; you end up consuming it yourself or sharing it with someone else; or somebody steals it from you. This is the definition of a perceptual mind. Don't do that, it says.

But lay up for yourselves treasures in Heaven, where neither moth nor rust doth corrupt, and where thieves do not break through nor steal... (Matthew 6:20) This is the certainty that in Heaven, which is full mind, you cannot lose, nothing can be taken from you, it's impossible to consume because there is no necessity for existence, and obviously you don't conserve and nothing can rot because you give it away. Laying it up in Heaven is the way Jesus teaches loving thoughts. Since mind is only thought, you store thoughts in Heaven rather than in limited perceptual relationships. Listen to what it says: But lay up for yourselves treasures in Heaven... Store in Heaven these thoughts.... where moth nor rust doth corrupt, and where thieves do not break through nor steal; For where your treasure is, there will your heart be also. (Matthew 6:21) We talked about the fact that cause and effect are not apart. If your heart is on earth, you will treasure the things of earth. If your heart is determined to seek the Kingdom, you will find it. Why? The power of your mind has directed you to seek the holiness.

The light of the body is the eye... Imagine this, He's talking about the Holy Spirit. He's talking about body enlightenment. *The light of the body is the eye...* What are we going to do? We are going to enlighten the body! Jesus, the great initiate, was aware of the transformation; the perfect, was aware of the transformation of the body: Know ye not that ye must be born again? (John 3:3) is directing you in this manner.

The light of the body is the eye; if therefore thine eye be single, thy whole body shall be full of light. Full of whole perceptual consciousness – not split up, not fractured, not in darkness. Not looking through a mirror darkly, but reflecting the wholeness of the Holy Spirit contained in the Jerusalem, the temple, of your reality. Now listen, it really gets good: But if thine eye is evil, thy whole body shall be full of darkness. That means either you see or you don't. If therefore the light that is in thee be darkness... Now it doesn't say that if the light that is in you is dark, it says that if the light that is in you is *darkness.* What a strange thing to say. Why? The power of mind is yours and you will be contained within your own darkness shining your light. Can you hear that? If therefore the light that is in thee be darkness, how great is that darkness! (Matthew 6:23) How great is the darkness of your light if it is dark. It literally means you can't see. How great is that darkness through the power of your light reflecting on itself in its limited associations of perception. That's what this says.

No man can serve two masters: for either he will hate the one, and love the other; or else he will hold to the one, and despise the other. (Matthew 6:24) This happens inevitably if you try to be loyal to somebody in your own perception. Somehow you will despise the message of your wholeness. The whole admonition of Jesus is this: **you cannot serve God and mammon**. There is no in-between. This is the whole *Course In Miracles.* Be thankful that this is so. What is *mammon?* Somebody says mammon is money. Mammon is perceptual mind. Mammon is the idea of accumulation, of shortage, of the need to exist separate from wholeness.

Therefore I say unto you, take no thought for your life, what ye shall eat, or what ye shall drink; nor yet for your body, what ye shall put on. Is not the life more than meat, and the body than raiment? (Matthew 6:25) How lovely. Isn't life more than food? Isn't life more than existing, more than consuming? Isn't life more than consuming in order not to die? Isn't the body more than clothing – more than just a bunch of thought forms that you are holding together – the clothing, the appearance of the thought form that you have projected from yourself?

Behold the fowls of the air; for they sow not, neither do they reap, nor gather into barns; yet your heavenly Father feedeth them. Are ye not much better than they? A bird knows itself to be whole and perfect. Ready, here's a key sentence: ***Which of you by taking thought can add one cubit unto his stature?*** (Matthew 6:26-27) What this says is *come as you are.* If you are contained within your perceptual limitation, no matter how much you worry or try to reorganize it, you cannot change your stature. You cannot grow from what you have ordained yourself to be. What's the solution to that? Stop worrying, and come as you are, created perfectly in the name of God. Which of you by taking thought can add one cubit unto his stature? Why worry? Why do you worry about these forms.

Consider the lilies of the field, how they grow; they toil not, neither do they spin; and yet I say unto you, that even Solomon in all his glory was not arrayed like one of these. (Matthew 6:27-29) This is the certainty of the non-necessity for you to define yourself. It's the whole idea that you are perfect in the sight of God as He created you rather than having to put on the clothes of form, rather than having to exist to defy death to pretend that you are not that whole self. This is lesson 76 of *A Course In Miracles* – and all of the other lessons where you are directed to give up your limited thought form associations and to come home and be with God.

Wherefore, if God so clothe the grass of the field, which today is, and tomorrow is cast into the oven... That means that no matter passes away, it is eternal, ... *shall he not much more clothe you, O ye of little faith?* That is a direct statement to you that you must be willing finally to accept the certainty of this message. Therefore take no thought, saying, what shall we eat? or, what shall we drink? or, wherewithal shall we be clothed? That is the whole idea that the perceptual mind holds onto its previous relationships, gathers together its necessities within the time framework, and lives in the past and in the future. The whole teachings of Jesus in the Course are for you to stop doing that. Begin to relinquish and become whole. For after all these things do the Gentiles seek... Gentiles in this sense means perceptual mind. Jew, as defined in the early tradition, meant perfect or perfected mind. King of the Jews means king of those who have come to perfect mind and express it. A Gentile was separate from God. This is not in the terms of the religion of Gentile and Jew... . for your heavenly Father knoweth that ye have need of all these things. But seek ye first the Kingdom of God, and his righteousness, and all these things shall be added unto you. Notice it says *added*, not becoming a part of you. If you have sought the Kingdom of God, you have found it. You stay here for a moment, then, on the earth, but not of it. You just add up these little things that are necessities through your own wholeness of mind to keep this message as the Christ for just this moment. Isn't that lovely? Take therefore no thought for the morrow; for the morrow shall take thought for the things of itself. Tomorrow will worry about its own things – that's the same as today worrying about its own things. Isn't that lovely. You'll notice that Jesus and all whole minds inevitably attempt to show you that time is not sequential and the manner in which you come to know that all of this consciousness around you is not moving, as in Chapter 13 in the Course, is by relinquishing your past and future associations. Take therefore no thought for the morrow, for the morrow shall take thought for the things of itself. Sufficient unto the day is the evil thereof. (Matthew 6:30-33)

Two thousand years ago, translated, discussed, analyzed, but still the same single whole thing that you as a new Christian now declare. In you is all the power of Heaven and by the decision of your mind to relinquish your associations – literally giving up the world, you can come to know the unreality of this. This is the declaration of this message. This is what you, now, in this time/space have come together to declare. Is Jesus of Nazareth here with us now? Where did you think He was? Jesus of Nazareth, this whole thought form, is you in the essence of the unhealed man coming healed each moment with the certainty of your mind, undergoing the transfiguration or the change of your mind to the light of this reality through the gathering of the light rays, through the contagion of the passion of your declaration now as you are in this room. You are dreaming a true dream; a dream still, but perfected by the brightness that shines now from this new association of yours so that all the thoughts coming out from you express the wholeness, the full endeavor of the free Christian whose mind can now choose to *be* rather than the necessity of the formulation of a thought from outside itself.

I'm grateful for the privilege of being able to come here. It's an incredible manifestation of reality in my mind to be with awakening minds. I know that most of you now remember that all of this has occurred before. It's impossible that we do anything in our perceptions that was not a part of our whole thought form relationship. We don't meet strangers. We merely meet previous thought forms and/or future thought forms redesigned in our minds to shine wholly by our creative purpose. That's what you're doing and that's what is spreading around the world. The joy and happiness that you're experiencing now is the fulfillment of your function. You are taking the power of your mind, which is all there is in the universe, and making application of it in your perceptual purpose. You have come to know who you are, and as you increasingly declare it, the doubt that you experienced at the initial schism leaves you in time as you advance to the light.

In the beginning was the Word,
and the Word was with God, and the Word was God.
The same was in the beginning with God.
All things were made by him;
and without him was not any thing made that was made.
In him was life; and the life was the light of men.
And the light shineth in darkness;
and the darkness comprehended it not.

CHAPTER THREE

Genesis

We don't really know who we are or how we got here. Since the beginning of man, man has been an expression of someone who was determined to authenticate, culturally/racially, his relationship with the universe. That's what you are. That's what this is.

Let's do Bible. Let's say that this then, is a testimony of man in his determination to establish his relationship with what he thinks he is or with the universe. Is that what this is? I'm asking you. Is that what this is? What do you mean you don't know? You know it is a story about man. It's a testimony. I don't care what you think this is. You call it a Bible. What is a Bible but a reference point from which you direct the attentions of the association of yourself. You are looking for something difficult in this. The fact of the matter is you have come here and have established a reference, a Bible, in order to attempt to determine a purpose for what you are doing here. You call that a religion. What do you care what you call it? You are the only thing I know of that does that. Because, obviously, you are the only thing that I know of that apparently is contained within his own relationship of cause and effect as a human being.

In that particular way, since the beginning of time, which is nothing but an historic reference of associations of the memory of man, you have told stories about yourself."In the beginning, God created heaven and earth." What an astonishing idea. You remember this: that idea is not in the mind of God, it is in the mind of man. It is man that is saying: God created heaven and earth. Obviously, if God created heaven and earth, if there is a universal mind, He would have no problem. He probably wouldn't even have to say it. Why would He have to say: I am the creator of heaven. Who would there be not to know that? Obviously, we have a situation –whatever we may be in the so-called evolutionary process of associations of time –with a necessity to establish a purpose for our reality and to share that purpose in the limitations invoked in the practice of our own historic references of ourselves. I'm not interested in whether you call this the Christian Bible or any other historic reference. What do I care? Whenever you go back into references of associations, actually you have a story about yourself and about the beginning of the world, and about the first man and the first woman. I find that fascinating. And you use it as a Bible, or a reference of the associations of man in a determination to find your own purpose. What's wrong with that? I think it's lovely. That's what this book is!

Two things we're facing if you really would care to look at it. First of all, man has obviously invented in his mind association, through whatever fundamental needs were inherent in himself as a conceptual association of cause and effect, with the necessity for a Creator with more power than he had in association with himself. This is a very strange development. What he actually says is: there is a power in the universe that authenticates my relationship with myself. He doesn't say that, but that's what he would have to do, because he finds himself in this condition. So the invention of a God or an entirety of association that you can request beneficial results in your own relationship is a phenomenal occurrence. If you look at yourself as an animal, you would say it's an animal that invented a God. How lovely.

So we don't know where we've come from, but let's agree that: "In the beginning God created the heaven and the earth." Here's the fundamental necessity of you as an individual in your own mind. This then has to be a story about us. I don't care where you think this story leads you in regard to what you believe this says as a story. Obviously this is a story –the whole Old and New Testament are nothing but stories. They're telling you stories about man's relationship with man. You then take the story and evoke from it the gratification of your own association with yourself based on the terms of reference that you can use to tell your own story. If you care to look at it fundamentally, how else would man describe himself except narratively? Let me see you talk to me without being narrative. If I threw religion out of it, I could teach this way. Obviously everybody you meet is a narration of the Old Testament, and the New Testament —or Christ came to life or He didn't —or my mother and dad were Adam and Eve. I don't care. Somewhere you're going to tell the story of yourself in association with yourself. I want you to say something to me that is not narrative. You can't because we're standing in an association and we're constantly telling stories about ourselves, and we're trying to determine whether the stories are true or not. They're stories to start out with. They are attempts to symbolize relationships that we have with each other. Isn't that amazing? That's just a true thing! It's impossible to have concepts without associations of symbols. You can't do it. It's what consciousness is.

Here you are trapped in a story. To authenticate yourself, you have a history or reference of your own genetic makeup —your mother and dad and your grandfather and maybe you search back to the 15th century. You go back wherever you can in order to continue the continuity of the maintenance of yourself in a story in time. You are a twice told tale. You are telling the story over and over again. What is the truth behind the story? The truth behind the story is where you utilize the story form of your own involvement in your own mind in a cognition that all man really attempts to do is define his relationship with a single, universal mind. I don't know how else to describe it.

Let's do a couple of parallels. The story in Genesis says very simply that God created heaven and earth and that he had a couple called Adam and Eve. From then on, the stories are not too much concerned with Adam and Eve, but only with the offspring of Adam and Eve. Suppose I wanted to tell you the story of the Old Testament in what I will term an esoteric manner. What does that mean, esoteric? Does it mean there are hidden meanings behind Adam and Eve and chewing on the apple, and the serpent? What it means is there are hidden meanings behind everything, and that all of the meanings that you bring into the association are meanings that you want to correlate in your own mind in regard to it if you had admitted to me that you are nothing but a story of yourself. But the problem you have with that is the broader the range of your association in regard to the factoring of your own mind, the less explicit you will be in the determination of the symbols. There isn't anything wrong with saying God made a man and a woman and he put them in a garden with a tree and a real serpent came down. But when you are done with it, what do you have? You have a limitation of the creation of your own mind. No one does that. They attempt to do it, but they can't do it without beginning to decide if there is another purpose. And the other purpose would have to be the totality of the image, that is, the serpent then becomes evil, and therefore all serpents are evil, or however the symbolic relationship occurs.

There's no question that the historic testimony of this continuum of association, what we call our DNA, our genetic memories –as we evolve it in genealogy –is adequately described in the Old Testament. Let's try it. We have Adam and Eve. When we're dealing with Adam and Eve we immediately are presented with two offspring. Forget us for a minute. Because actually we have nothing to do with Cain and Abel. We just think we do. Cain and Abel are the first indications of the association of the totality of potential, which is Abel and Cain, which is the mind of man in association with himself. I know you're going to say: well, that's just the story. I'm going to make this as fundamental as I can. The only attempts that were ever made in the separation were to establish a continuity or relationship between love, which is what God is, and intellect or separation that pertains to man's determination to define love in his own relationship of separation. That's a description of Cain. Obviously the consequences of Cain, which is man's intellect, would be to destroy his heart relationship with each other, and dominate through the means of the progression of his own intellect to the certainty of what you would call space-time relationships, without the totality of Abel. So what happens in the story: Obviously Cain kills his brother. I don't know how else it could be described to you, because obviously they were both brothers of God. Cain kills Abel. When God says: Cain, where is your brother? Cain says: Am I my brother's keeper? (Gen 4:9) He has nothing at all to do with the totality of his association. Geographically, what you would call historically in the reference then, we have a condition called Cainism. We have a condition where man,

32

in his capacity of symbolic relationship, is remaining in the focus, using the power of God to express himself in cause and effect relationships. In the references mystically, the description of Cain is the description of Atlantis. Atlantis is the intellectual capacity of man to associate separately from the heart. Obviously Atlantis would be destroyed by *la mer* (the sea), or the condition of illusion of the necessity for the love of God. So what is God's answer to the death of Abel? He makes another heart. What is the name of the next heart? I'm doing references of man. I just did 50,000 years that didn't work genetically. We couldn't be Cains, it wouldn't work. Biologically all we are doing is turning over for a million years a means where we can combine the heart or love of God with our own minds.

Who are we offspring of? In the Bible. Who? Seth! When Cain slew Abel, the first thing God says to Cain is you can't stay here, you have to go out east of Eden and be in the Land of Nod. So Cain is asleep and lives the illusion of Atlantis contained within his own mind. Have you heard of the Land of Nod –it's east of Eden contained within the potential of the illusion.

So now we have no heart. So we need a better combination of associations of Abel and Cain, and the next line in the Bible says that God made Seth. Adam has Seth, it doesn't say God made him. Adam has Seth. So we're offspring of Seth. Homo sapiens is a Seth association. That period could be a million years, a thousand years, I don't care. In the meantime, we have Cain out east of Eden asleep. How many thousands of years have passed? What difference does that make? Remember what we're talking about fundamentally here, we're attempting to describe ourselves in relationship with the things that we are contained within our own selves, and we have to use symbols to do it. What I'm offering you is a connection between the historic references that you will read in literature and in so-called mystical artifacts. The truth of them will be contained in the history of yourself as a testimony to the contents of the memory of evolving man.

The Old Testament is a description of the entire condition of man, not only in relationship to himself as Seth offspring, which would be a period of Homo sapiens, but as the failures that occurred biologically within man as he attempted it. So here now suddenly we have Seth. He's working pretty good. He works fine down on through generations all the way to where he's not going to work any more. We get to Noah, and things are not right. I'm talking now in the broadest sense. Suddenly, we are faced with the totality of associations –it's all in here, it lists generation after generation of man keeping track of himself. In the meantime, Atlantis has been destroyed and we are on some sort of dry land. Pure love obviously could not survive on dry land and has returned to the sea, which is what the dolphin is. A dolphin is pure love without the capacity to exist in the form association. All it does is love. If you looked at a bank of dolphins, how much they love you, they will have an historic reference. What I call the archetypal dolphins that don't participate in the play, are a totality of a description of the Old Testament –including their love and return here and their communication at other levels of form association. So let's let the love be for a while because obviously it's a form of illusion or *la mer* (the sea) to you. Atlantis had to be destroyed simply because it had no love in it. So now we're left with a condition that was not going to gratify as rapidly as could be determined within the continuum of associations the potential that could be realized in your return from time to eternity. What did we need? A flood. We had to wipe it out again. We had to retain the parts of it that would best benefit us –what you call historically, what you call evolutionary-wise –two of everything, or combinations, so that we could literally start a new race or condition of man. This is precisely what happened.

Suddenly we have a whole story of how the ark lands and I'm not going to do the story. But now we have a condition that we are getting pretty recent. We're discovering that genetically man has refined and refined and refined his associations within himself so that when I tell you that we are all from the same genetic strain, I'm talking about very recently. The other associations, whether you call them Ape Man, Cave Man, it doesn't matter –are obviously not a part of the continuum in which we find ourselves. In that regard, we are extremely recent. An article you might want to read in the science literature yesterday in determining the DNA has absolutely made a discovery that the entire condition of man had to be reduced to less than ten thousand total inhabitants on earth –actually it goes back to Lucy, the original strain –but there's a variance in the strain, and they're determined that all of us genetically come from that very small post-flood condition. It's fascinating to know that not only are we very recent, but we are a refinement of space/time. We are so close to each other, that the genetic DNA between a so-called European and a Chinaman, which is not really indistinguishable, is closer than a gorilla in one section of the jungle has with another gorilla that's 50 miles away. Their genetic strain is more separate. What we're actually saying is what I've been telling you, we're all alike. We are so recent in the images of ourselves, that we're just looking at our own genetic memories. Isn't that fascinating.

So now we've got ourselves past the flood, and on we go. So we have the Old Testament that's telling us a story of the totality of man in his relationship with the world. Or tell me another story. Why are we dealing with the Old Testament? Because the Old Testament is an example of man's condition in cause and effect relationships. Obviously there would be a necessity, found repeatedly in the Old Testament, of an intercession by a consciousness association who combined all of the so-called attributes of man in his relationship with God. You call that Christ. I'm not concerned about what you call it. But what purpose would you have here within space/time, having invented a God within your own mind, that you would not realize the certainty that you are that. That's what you're being offered.

How good is your mind at taking analogies, like I just did with you —now that analogy is alive to me in my mind. Here's what *A Course In Miracles* teaches you: it teaches you to take all of your conceptual associations within your own story and let them always mean more than they meant to you before. Do you understand what I just said? Why don't you give yourself more meaning? Why is that hard to understand if you have already determined you're going to be the meaning you are anyway. Obviously you must be asking for a lot less than you are because you've already told me that God made you perfect. Just as obviously you're operating within the principles of your own conceptual association. And just as obviously you have the power which you exercise in your own mind to define yourself. All the Course really says that if you need to define yourself, why do you define yourself as a rotting carcass sitting in a pew in Baraboo. That's the only question. It's not that you're not going to define yourself because your condition is a definition. The practice of the miracle is nothing but the momentary release of the old definition of yourself without the necessity to repeat again and again with the new genetic you, the new man, the New Testament, derives with the certainty that you are whole as God created you.

Where is the fear that this association has in regard to this? It's the admission that it is the cause of the world. That's what it's afraid of. It has no intention of being responsible for the thousands of people that are starving. It can't. It closes itself down in, lives within the very limitation of its own genetic memories. Where is its dolphin? In the sea. It couldn't stand it. If things are creations of its own mind, it would be forced to look at the fact that it is killing the things it loves. I'm doing Atlantis here. Obviously if it truly is as I am indicating to you, if this world is only your own mind, you obviously must be killing the things that you love because you are in a condition of killing. This is the whole teaching of Jesus of Nazareth. All it says is: give everything up and come on home and love. You have heard it said an eye for an eye. (Matthew 5:38) Throw that all out and come home. Obviously you don't do that, you sit here and get cancer and die. All we're telling you is don't do that. Somewhere the decision has to be made by you based on the totality of you of the offering I give you to the ultimate relationship you must have if you're in an evolutionary process. You're just going to have to emerge from the chaos of cause and effect and be a whole mind as you were created by God. I went to a funeral yesterday and there was no life in it at all. Just as the funerals you go to, and that body is dead and all the other bodies say what a wonderful thing that body was. What nonsense. Nothing dies. All of this is only in your own mind. Nothing really leaves. What a situation to find yourself in!

So we got past Seth and the dove came and sat on Noah's head and we've got a big rainbow that says God is not going to destroy the earth anymore. All that meant is now we've got what we need. It meant that at last we've got a species that could see a rainbow and could see a dove on the head. That's exactly what happened. That's what Jesus describes when He describes the physical awakening. He sees rainbows and the dove lands on your head. There's a lot in the Old Testament. You can get to Isaiah and you can have a lot of fun with it.

Mostly it's just a description of man's condition with man. But contained within this very current reference, I'm talking about 40,000 years, are all of the possible combinations of the perfected necessity of Homo sapiens. I don't care who he is, the genetic relationship of that body is identical to all the other bodies. This is the whole teaching. That's what constitutes you as the savior of the world. That's what makes you the Christ –Homo sapiens. That definition of yourself in the totality of your relationship through the accumulation of the forms of your DNA make you able to do that. And you're doing it, aren't you? So somewhere you know that this is true.

If it is true, if there is such a thing as a history, it would be obvious that if there is a unifying association, that all history must be contained in you. The question is not that, the question is why would you live in your old history when you can just as well live in your future history? Do you understand the evolution? That's *A Course In Miracles.* It says simply: you invented time so don't sequence it. Time is an invention of the form of the associations of your own mind. If you sequence it, you will be trapped in the Old Testament. You will keep telling the same story over and over again. But if any association, which is just contained within your own mind, was resurrected in the certainty of the truth, it would have to be you, because He's the same as you. Jesus Christ of Nazareth is you. I don't care what you call Him –he can have any different memories he wants, but in the correlation of the memories, he must reach the conclusion of love. You cannot not reach the conclusion of eternal love and happiness. That's what he wants to be. Not only is that what he is, but somewhere that's what he wants to be. So for you to suffer the conflict of the old covenant, which was the eye for an eye covenant, makes no sense at all.

Don't sequence your time. All you're telling me in this new association is that you are no longer sequencing time. I can tell that you are living in knowledge. All you are saying is never mind that, if I'm going to remember, I might as well remember the whole thing, because I have in me that capacity. That's completely individual. Obviously you are going to have to have the experience yourself within your own body. If you look at how small the earth is, it wouldn't bother you at all. Look at how small you are compared to the universe. You're contained within that little association. This genetic memory that you are experiencing is nothing but your own mind, contained within the cognition of the relationship of space/time. You have nothing to fear because there is no such thing as fear. There cannot be such a thing as fear unless you are separated from God. Since you are the one that told me that there is a God and wholeness, it must be you that knows of the separation. If you are determined to stay fearful and allow the dolphins to stay in *la mer* (the sea—the illusion), I can't do anything about it because all directions of your left brain association will dictate terms that must be acceptable to your right, based on your determination to authenticate your relationships within the historic references of the limitations of your Old Testament.

Finally I get to the point where Jesus says there's nothing else to say. The reason that is so is because you are starting to communicate.

So this is the testimony or the history of us in a genetic relationship with each other. You say: why am I in this tradition? Why do I have to be in this tradition? It makes absolutely no difference where you are, you're the one that's in there. I'm only speaking of the manner in which you apply your mind in association with the symbols which are inventions of your mind. If you want to do an analogy with me, I'll use the ark, if you want to do a perfect analogy of cubits of the ark with the human body, I'll be happy to support you and show you that's exactly true. I'd have to get you to admit we were talking in microcosm. You are so determined to express yourself in wholeness that you have constructed a body which is the geographic entirety of the earth. Are you aware of that? Have you read the details of the human body in relationship with the cubits and how it's directly associated with the containment of your own genetic memory? This is the Tigris and Euphrates (legs), the cradle of civilization is what you call your first chakra. Civilization began at the source of the Tigris and Euphrates and spread into Egypt and there are geographic descriptions showing Egypt with the Tigris and Euphrates which is exactly what the human body is. Where did you get your capacity to do that? Is it true that your body is that? Yes, it's true. Microcosmically, the distance between that association and Jerusalem is the totality of the relationship between Egypt and Jerusalem. There's nothing outside of you! I'm telling you that you are not a body, you are free. But certainly if you are going to be a body, why don't you be a total one? If you are going to be a body of association, why not be a whole body association since the whole body is what you are.

You can draw me all the stars you want, and you can do the horoscopes, you can have each one of them represent a story in the circle of your own atonement and you can describe yourself as a Pisces or an Aquarius –you have to be a Pisces before you can be an Aquarius –how the hell do I know? You have to fish for men before you can have your own enlightenment. You like it when you do this. I'm not taking anything away from you. As you evolve your capacity of miracle mindedness, you begin to make use of everything. You don't bind yourself into the old relationship. You walk along and say: I wonder what that is. I'll tell you what it is, it's you. You are trapped in a little place in your own mind and you're beginning to have the experience of enlightenment. Oh, is that like the dove landing on my head? What would you like it to be? If you try to replicate it, the dove surer than hell will just crap on your head! What good is the symbol if I trap a dove and set it on my head? Yet this is what the human being does in an attempt to replicate the symbols rather than allow them to mean what your expanding consciousness lets them mean. Ultimately, this is the same as Lesson 130 –the two worlds cannot communicate. Each time you release the necessity for the symbol relationship of yourself, you become symbiotic in the totality of your own mind.

All I'm offering you is your own mind. Let everything that you do be a part of your awakening process and you couldn't possibly fail. Why? You already awoke. I love this book (Bible). Obviously this is a history of you up until your time of resurrection. It includes your resurrection. It's in here. Your Easter is in here. You come here and die and crucify yourself, doing the same thing over and over again when He is Risen. He is Risen INDEED! We're Christians here. Happy Easter.

That's the Old Testament for today. Wait until I get into Leviticus. I'll do Exodus first. Wow. They almost got back to Jerusalem. Notice I said "almost." Forty years can't quite make it. He never makes it. He gets out of Egypt, though. So he's trapped somewhere between Egypt and Jerusalem. All of us finally are trapped somewhere in that 40 years. Let's call it 40 days and get it over with. Now we just call it 40 hours.

How about calling it four minutes. Obviously it's any period or as long as it takes to go from Egypt to Jerusalem. How long? Forty days. But you're over the hump. Cain is sleeping over in Nod. You don't have to worry about him. The Cain in you cannot exist in this association. He's asleep. Now the love of you is in *la mer* (the sea) awaiting the maturity of you and your Atlantis has been destroyed. So you have everything to look forward to because it was you all the time. The discovery you make in your own illumination is that it was always you. I've got you so squeezed in your own genetic relationship that you can see that we're all the same. It took the entire three billion years of earth –you're going to read this article that says it cannot be more than 10,000 years –it's all-encompassed into us. The whole world!

Numbers and Deuteronomy gets a little more into mysteries. Joshua will be mystic revelation. Judges, Ruth, I & 11 Samuel –history, I & 11 Kings, I & 11 Chronicles –will be a little better, Ezra, Nehemiah, Ester, Job, Psalms, Proverbs, Ecclesiastics –will be "vanity always vanity." I'm doing the Old Testament. Are you up on your Old Testament? After you Ecclesiastics –which is Atlantis, you get Song of Solomon –which is the greatest love story ever told. So much that they had to expunge it from what it actually said, it got too risqué. Your love of God got so passionate in Song of Solomon that they had to ban it, did you know that? It comes after Ecclesiastics which is the teacher, and the teacher is just expressing what many of you Course teachers have expressed –your inability to teach it. You say: "vanity, vanity, always vanity," but you don't know how to get out of it. The Song of Solomon is how to get out of it.

They kicked some of it out in the 5th century, some of the esoteric books have been taken out. You wonder how Song of Solomon could be in there. That's because of a mystical rabbi, Solomon deLeon, who went into a cave and disappeared into light incidentally. He fought the battle of leaving some of the esoteric books in here. He said: I don't know what it says, but I know it has got to be in there. Isn't that nice to know?

CHAPTER FOUR

Ask And It Shall Be Given

As the savior of the world, dedicated to the certainty that the universal mind is singular and you are that, the frustration will always be the necessity to teach to the perceptual mind in the first place. The perceptual mind is inherently demonstrating its own capacity of judgmental association based on the terms it has established within its own self.

If you don't correlate the devices that you are using to come to this, you will simply let your eye become one. Let's use Jesus, or you –you come into a situation and perform an apparent miracle. It is a performance of reassociation of what was previously sick and now is well. All performances of perceptual mind require a correspondence of the situation in order to verify the occurrence of the performance. The mind is designed specifically to suffer a relief from conflict in the verification of a performance based on the power of perception to perform. The denial of you as a performer is literally a denial of the miraculous healing of God, or a definition of you in your capacity to keep your cause and effect separate. Through the demonstration of this miracle, I am showing you that you are perfect as God created you.

What is the greatest fear of this world? Your Miracle Healing Center. It is a total threat to the establishment of man. It is afraid to be healed. It is afraid to be well. If it were well, it wouldn't have an identity of its own. It's afraid of totality. ***It is very important that the Miracle Healing Center be taught as individual atonement.***

Trying to teach it as cultural establishment re-identity will be what they'll attempt to force on you to make you come into an established association. If you do that, they can formulate a doctrine concerning the method by which you heal. ***The key to this is that you heal by no method at all***. The method is nothing but a distance between the cause and the effect that will retain the necessity for the verification of the sickness. This seems real simple, and it is real simple for you perceptually. But I want you to understand that I'm talking in a literal sense. I'm saying that we can create a healing, we can bring about a reassociation of the factoring of form to the single dedication of the power of our minds not to identify with the world. That's an active determination of faith. You cannot do it without letting faith come into it, because any activity of your perceptual mind will be an attack on reality. It doesn't seem as though it is. But any aspect that you introduce between a direct cause and effect relationship will cause you to continue to construct various associations.

All of the New Testament is an expression of the battle between what Jesus is saying and what they are going to insist that He is saying. The whole New Testament, page after page, they are going to determine what He's saying, and He's always saying: I'm not saying that. He can't do it by a direct correspondence with the association because He would be in Heaven. If He says: I am the savior of the world and we are in Heaven together, it is accomplished. Because of the drama of the individual associations, He must speak in physical metaphor. He must speak in metaphor of a correspondence of the individual perceptual mind's determination to let its causation be a totality of universal mind and that can be done, and must be done, in an allegory of the identity of the self proclamation –that is, the autonomy of your mind. It can't be done in any other way. But you will get the result that you ask for. Faith is asking for the totality and not interpreting immediately the results. Don't let the aspects of the situation distract you from the certainty of what I am telling you.

Can you imagine what they say about what you'll be doing: They will say, *Course in Miracles* students are healing, but they're using the devil to heal. You think you can open a Center here and have the admission that God is doing the healing? It's not possible. They will find every means they can to verify the association of your capacity to heal within the limited frame of what they are. In a very real way, God healing is the devil to them. There's no cause for your healing. What is more evil than the destruction of your own causation? The idea that no method is applied is totally evil. The greatest threat to the medical establishment will be your Healing Center. The more miracles that occur, the less tolerated it will be. It is literally the destruction of the need to die and stay in the association. What a terrible situation to be in. Fortunately there's no reality in it. Unfortunately, they think there is.

When Jesus went out and taught to the recognition of his own awakening process, inevitably the correspondence of His whole mind began to manifest miracles. It cannot *not*. You have manifested miracles in this association. You have been taught not to credit your association with yourself in the miracle, and allow it to come from the natural reality of what you are. This is the total dilemma of Jesus of Nazareth teaching the world, and axiomatically, himself, in regard to the credit He will take in association with the miracle. He is very much aware that in miracle working, there is no such thing as a miracle worker, but a definition of labor involved in miraculous healing, will cause the necessity for a separation of the cause and the effect. It cannot *not* without the admission that the sickness and the remedy are the same.

Luke, who is a recounter –Luke can really irritate you because he doesn't recognize levels of thought. He has a tendency simply to report what's said, and it's all over the place. He presents a particularly tough teaching because the things that Jesus said, for example, about the Pharisees are very difficult when not looked at in the totality of the context of a whole mind addressing another mind. He didn't want anything to do with them. Here's a little Luke. Here's a correspondence written out that goes with the Lord's Prayer. Once the mind evolves an ability to find correspondence in the symbol relationship of its definition of itself, it will do it in a continuing effort. This (piece of paper) says: Heaven (Father) - pituitary; name - pineal; will - thyroid; evil - thymus; debts - solar plexus; temptation - lyden; bread - gonads. Absolutely true.

They ask Jesus in Luke, chapter 11, for a single prayer, how to pray, and He gives them the Lord's Prayer, which is lovely, you may interpret it any way you want. All it really says is that God's will is done on earth as it is in Heaven, and there's nothing you're going to be able do about it. Then He talks about the necessity of the admission of the need of your brother in the correspondence with your need. A guy comes to your house and asks for help, won't you give it to him? At what point do you decide its more valuable to hold your relationships with yourself rather than give them away? That's the context.

I say unto you, Though he will not rise and give him, because he is his friend, yet because of his importunity he will rise and give him as many as he needeth. (Luke 11:8) It is impossible in any situation you're not going to get exactly what you need if you don't bring other aspects of the situation and demand a correspondence within your own mind.

And I say unto you, Ask, and it shall be given you; seek, and ye shall find; knock, and it shall be opened unto you. (Luke 11:9) This is an active statement of your determination to return to God. It cannot be denied you because the factoring is contained within your own mind. But you must be constant in the so-called result that you want based on your own association. This is chapter 18 in the Course. Don't be faithless to the correspondence of the realization of the perfection of your own mind in what apparently has been projected outside of you. All that could possibly be is what you have determined you want it to be to hold the conflict of your own mind.

For everyone that asketh receiveth; and he that seeketh findeth; and to him that knocketh it shall be opened. (Luke 11:10) That's simply a statement that cause and effect are not apart. You cannot ask for something and not get it. Your problem is that you are not certain what to ask for because you don't know who you are. Not knowing who you are, you continually ask for reassociations of the aspects of the correspondence of your own mind. And you get that. But God would not give you a symbol of what you have asked for unless you insist on symbolizing a relationship to what is objective to your mind.

If a son shall ask bread of any of you that is a father, will he give him a stone?... No, he'll give him bread. Yet it appears to you when you ask for something you don't get what you ask for. You don't know what to ask for. All this really says is you're going to get exactly what you ask for.... or if he ask a fish, will he for a fish give him a serpent? (Luke 11:11) Will he give him something he doesn't want? You are getting what you ask for. You ask for love and you appear to get evil. You are not asking for love, you are asking for evil or it would be impossible that you get it. You cannot *not* get what you're asking for. That's fundamentally rejected. But it is fundamentally true with the reasonableness of an association of the mind contained within itself and being directed by the outcome that it wants to receive in a situation. Or if he shall ask an egg, will he offer him a scorpion? (Luke 11:12) That's an interesting analogy.

Now He's going to say you're using so little of the power of your mind when God wants to give you everything: If ye then, being evil, (you're separated) know how to give good gifts unto your children... You're searching for happiness within your own separation, don't you think God in His totality also wants His children to be happy in the certainty of what He is? Is God's mind different than yours? It's impossible that God's mind is different than yours. You are God's mind.... how much more shall your Heavenly Father give the Holy Spirit to them that ask him? (Luke 11:13) God doesn't give, the spirit of your totality with yourself gives to God.

And he was casting out a devil, and it was dumb. And it came to pass when the devil was gone out, the dumb spake, and the people wondered. (Luke 11:14) It doesn't say that the devil caused the dumbness, it says that the devil was the act of being dumb. Quite literally when you see God you're often struck dumb. Dumbness is a denial of God. But some of them said, He casteth out devils through Beelzebub, the chief of the devils. And others, tempting him, sought of him a sign from heaven. (Luke 11:15-16) Wow! Walk on my swimming pool. But he, knowing their thoughts... He could not *not* know what they were doing because obviously everything they did was designed *not* to admit to who they were. An astonishing idea. What He says is if you believe that healing comes from evil, it will come from evil. But the idea that evil would heal is a house divided against itself. That's exactly what this says. In other words the guy says you are healing evil-ly, what he's saying is all healing is evil. This has to be distinguished in the form of division or judgment which must cause conflict within the house association.

Every kingdom divided against itself is brought to desolation; and a house divided against a house faileth. (Luke 11:17) Any division of perception in correspondence with any other division cannot succeed because it is what failure is. It is non-creative by the nature of its structure. If Satan also be divided against himself, how shall his kingdom stand?... Obviously. What He's saying is every situation is either totally good or it's totally bad. There is no in-between. Any division has no reality... . because ye say that I cast out devils through Beelzebub. And if I by Beelzebub cast out devils, by whom do your sons cast them out?... Is there something different in their healings? What He says is healing is healing, the hell with how it happens. The problem with how it happens is what evil is –separation or a determination that healing and reality aren't the same... . therefore shall they be your judges. (Luke 11:17-18) You have demanded that they judge you in a reciprocal association of the separation of your two houses. You cannot meet if you are determined to stay separate. You will judge without the realization that any judgment is the conflict of the unreality of separation.

But if I with the finger of God... I am using the finger of God, pointing at you in your wholeness, saying: this is my beloved son with whom I am well pleased. He points right at you: I Want You! Then you say: not me! You've been conscripted into the Glory Army. And there's a certain resistance to it. You've been drafted to do this. You would never do this willingly. But if I with the finger of God cast out devils, no doubt the kingdom of God is come upon you. It would have to be because I'm telling you it is so. When a strong man armed keepeth his palace, his goods are in peace. (Luke 11:21) If he allows any concern in regard to what he is in his relationship to God to intercede in his direction of where he is going with Heaven, his house will be divided automatically because he's divided power. If you divide power, you will get the result of the division without the admission of the totality of the situation. This is a problem many of you have had. The nice thing about Luke is right in the middle of a demonstration of a real occurrence he'll go with what Jesus says mystically. Many times you'll see that in our association together. I suddenly give you a parable of the physiological awakening. Or I'll give you a demonstration of an allegory of how we got into this. I have to do that because your minds are not capable of the admission of totality without some sort of conceptual association of what you are. Obviously the drama of objective reality is being played out in your dream. So it's not that it's veiled, it's that it need be veiled in order that you can hear it. That's what will occur right here. Here's what happens to you physically if you come here and don't manage to work through it.

He that is not with me is against me. (Luke 11:23) This is the crucial test of faithlessness compared to faith. If you are not with God, you are not "not with Him," you are against Him. That's an active resistance to the total social relationship of your capacity to heal and to demonstrate your love for each other. He that is not with me is against me; and he that gathereth not with me scattereth. (Luke 11:23) Amazing idea. Every time you deny, you literally associate with evil or death. It's a real tough idea.

When the unclean spirit is gone out of a man... This is when he undergoes a Holy Instant –that he has a relationship that transcends what he thought he was. For a moment Jesus is casting out unclean spirits, and the revelation of that reassociation in you and the correspondence of Jesus' mind literally heals that association. What does Jesus crucially say at that time –that you will say in your demonstration of healing in your Center? Go, and be no longer separated from God. Inevitably evil is connected with atonement and healing as the same thing. He will do that. This is an admission of the capacity to clean your temple momentarily and then literally fall back into sin –backsliding it's called –your capacity to demonstrate your own reality based on the autonomy of your need to die. When the unclean spirit is gone out of a man, he walketh through dry places, seeking rest; Just for a moment, he has used up all of the thoughts in his own mind since he depended on what you would call the illusion or wet places to correspond to himself, he is bereft of a capacity to establish himself in his own reality. He loses it for a moment. He doesn't know what to do... . he walketh through dry places seeking rest; and finding none, he saith, I will return unto my house whence I came out. (Luke 11:24) All of you are going through this. You keep looking back over the old situations trying to find some answers contained within the association that you had. The association that you had has been cleansed. It's not going to gratify you anymore. Here's the sentence: And when he cometh, he findeth it swept and

GETHSEMANE TO GALILEE: Master Teacher

garnished. (Luke 11:25) Actually it's garnished with God. That's just not acceptable because it's a place of total peace. If he comes back to his old home, it has been converted in time to a place of peace. If he does not go out and seek other conflict in his association, he will be whole with God. This is the body resurrection.

Then goeth he, and taketh to him seven other spirits more wicked than himself. (Luke 11:26) Can you hear that? This is mystical. They had to be more wicked than himself because he cleansed himself in his previous association. He now has to find something that he can identify within the chakras —obviously, there are seven of them —in his body association with himself in order to retain the tension or the separation of his capacity of darkness and darkness associations. They would have to be more wicked than himself because like Jesus says: I told you exactly what to do. You don't get less wicked, you always get more wicked. How could you get less wicked. You keep seeking for other ways to be wicked. They always eventually cause you more pain because you are searching for pain, and you are going to get what you are searching for. What an amazing idea.... he taketh to him seven other spirits more wicked than himself; and they enter in (he is possessed by his reassociation) and dwell there; and the last state of that man is worse than the first. (Luke 11:26) It doesn't get better. And this is handled pretty gently in this teaching. The fact of the matter is that if you use the power of your own mind, dictated by the terms of your own apparent revelation to God, in a demonstration to reestablish evil within your own continuum of thought, you will get the result of the additional power that you are using in order to demonstrate it. Can you hear that? There will be much gnashing of teeth. You are using the power of God to authenticate the association within your own mind. But it sure seemed good —look at all the power you could use temporarily. You are using the power temporarily to verify your own association or literally to attack reality within your own hallucination. It means nothing. Nothing is really happening here.

And it came to pass as he spake these things, a certain woman of the company lifted up her voice, and said unto him, Blessed is the womb that bare thee, and the paps which thou has sucked. (Luke 11:27) He's really not concerned about Mary's teats. All that really happens here is somebody is going to give him an idolization: Oh, what a great man you are –your mother must be wonderful, too. How are you able to do this? As a human being you sure learned a lot more than I've been able to learn. It is an exact denial of what He just said. How does He handle it? But he said, Yea rather, blessed are they that hear the word of God and keep it. (Luke 11:28) It doesn't have anything to do with me. Who cares what you think I am! God is. And you must be because that's all there is.

And when the people were gathered thick together, he began to say, This is an evil generation... Or a recognition of separation and a determination to hold on to it, the admission of first covenant. An evil generation is one that knows it is separated and searches for God within its separation capacity. That's what evil is, separation. It knows perfectly well it's separate, but verifies the separation in order to determine what God can be in the separation... . this is an evil generation: they seek a sign; and there shall no sign be given it, but the sign of Jonas the prophet. (Luke 11:29) And that's the sign of you might as well give up because you ain't going to get anywhere. They look for a sign of optimism concerning their continuing capacity to find the peace of God. And they will grasp at any straw and say this is the method I can use, I am succeeding at this. They cannot succeed. Not in this generation.

For as Jonas was a sign unto the Ninevites, so shall also the Son of man be to this generation. (Luke 11:30) That's another way of saying that you have had plenty of spiritual experiences, now it is time for the son of man to represent himself in a love that you are. Having been swallowed by the whale, spent three days in shit, risen up with all white hair, was a necessary part of Nineva, which was put down by Babylon. Nineva is the original what you would call aggregate structure of the Assyrian civilization. It is literally at the crotch of the Tigris and Euphrates. Nineva was a great seed that understood the fundamental concepts of its association. It was the original formulation of writing. It was really the original formulation of the possibility of communication. It then is distracted and overcome by Babylon in 600 BC. Babylon destroys it. Let's see what Jesus says about it.

For as Jonas was a sign unto Ninevites, so shall also the Son of man be to this generation. The queen of the south shall rise up in the judgment with the men of this generation, and condemn them...

That's literally a conversion of mother nature to Godliness. What is the queen of the south? Mother nature. The natural tendency for you to correspond in a reference of agriculture and gathering. The queen of the south is going to rise up. The memories you have of your maternal necessity of earthly correspondence, all of the genetic memory contained within your demonstrations of your capacity to exchange and be a part of this world. The queen of the south shall rise up in the judgment with the men of this generation, and condemn them: for she came from the utmost parts of the earth to hear the wisdom of Solomon; and behold, a greater than Solomon is here. (Luke 11:31) This is nothing but the demonstration of the capacity of an historic reference in time to come to its totality through the wisdom of the reassociation of Solomon or the wisdom mind. The idea that the nature gods, which is what *mother* is, were joined with Solomon, or a temple of wisdom contained in Jerusalem, is an extraordinary idea because the temple of Solomon is the admission of one god, demonstrated by the idolatry of the temple in the determination to retain it. But certainly past the capriciousness of the mother earth who only cares about survival and is totally indifferent to an aggregate reality, so that each cell is in conflict with every other cell. And greater than Solomon is here. He's talking about himself.

The men of Nineva shall rise up in the judgment with this generation, and shall condemn it; for they repented at the preaching of Jonas; and, behold, a greater than Jonas is here. (Luke 11:32) All Jonas ever taught was the total futility of earthly associations –it's going to crap on the good guys and the bad guys. There's no way that you can escape this. Having learned that, you are ready to undergo the experience. This is so obvious to me. When we teach in parables, we want you to bring about reassociations. I'm not concerned about the manner in which you organize your reassociations. The frustration that Jesus feels in this is He's certain that everybody knows about Nineva. He's certain they know the power of mystical associations in their own mind. You think that culture lived in some sort of isolation; it didn't. It was filled with demons and spirits, just as it is today.

Here's the physical resurrection: No man, when he hath lighted a candle (this is the original Christ), putteth it in a secret place, neither under a bushel, but on a candlestick, that they which come in may see the light. The light of the body is the eye; therefore when thine eye is single, thy whole body also is full of light. (Luke 11:33-34) That is about as mystical as you can get. If I have to explain this one to you, you don't belong in this room. He's teaching one-eyed-ness. That's the whole idea. With your concepts and your associations, you can't get enough light into your head to see the singularity of your association with God. The light of the body is the eye; therefore when thine eye is single, thy whole body also is full of light. Wow. The body resurrection... . but when thine eye is evil, thy body also is full of darkness. That's another way of saying you can't see two worlds. You're either totally dark in the association with your body or you'll be resurrected to the certainty of light.

Take heed therefore that the light which is in thee be not darkness. (Luke 11:35) What a strange sentence. I will not use my own past learning as the light to guide me now, because to you darkness is light. Light to you is any reasoning process by which you arrive at conclusions in association with yourself. If thy whole body therefore be full of light, having no part dark, the whole shall be full of light, as when the bright shining of a candle doth give thee light. (Luke 11:36) What an idea. That is nothing but the resurrection of the body.

Then there's all sorts of things about the necessity of the definition of the correspondence of man with his capacity to deny the apparent wholeness of what he is. The basis of the structure of this world is a timeful association of universal mind in a momentary inevitability of it to occur –not under the direction that you are determined to give it in the relationship with cause and effect. Let's carry that to the aspects of what you are going to try to do here.

Now you are going to open a Healing Center. You have to give it some sort of direction. The idea that you are teaching miraculous healing through a notification to Adam, or the individual association, that he is the totality of his own evilness contained within himself is precisely what we are teaching. If we teach it this way, you can open the Center where the concern of the association can be directed not to the therapy of death but the necessity for his identity, with the certainty of his creative power. You understand this! No therapy of any kind occurs in your Healing Center. This is not a place where solace, except in its entirety through the grace of God, is offered to the establishment.

Nothing will be more fearful to the conceptual establishment than that idea. Because what? It is literally the denial of the world. The process can be gentle, very simply because you have been allowed to present it to the association. It may well be that he will take what he can out of the revelatory experience that he has, spend 40 days in the wilderness, and succumb to the devil. What Jesus talks about is the original baptism of himself and the ordeal he underwent in His determination not to use this new-found power, not to be tempted to throw himself off a cliff. It's a part of what you are experiencing right now, since all temptation is only a determination to continue to attack God. It doesn't really make any sense. Don't be tempted to use the aspects of the association to become faithless in the faithful reassociation of what we are together. The beautiful thing about it is that it's happening all the time.

The miracle is nothing but an undoing of your determination to bring into faithfulness a variation in the direction of the goal which you have previously set in your mind. Be faithful to this goal of transformation —although all of the aspects of your mind will immediately present you with alternatives because your reality is based on the capacity of alternative relationships (ACIM chapter 19). Don't do that. And you will experience the miracle of healing. The retention of the memory of the necessity for the conflict, which is nothing but the human identity, is what the sickness is. Your Healing Center will teach individual outcome, not the phenomena. Let the phenomenon be what it is. That is what I just read you. They will just ask for more demonstrations.

One miracle is not any different from another. Why is that so? Sickness isn't real in the first place. What we're saying is what is sick is not real.

There is an advantage to making the connection to Christianity, very simply because if you don't you'll really have a problem. You are going to maintain that salvation has nothing to do with doctrine at all. Any correspondence of community is not what salvation is. That's the teachings of Jesus of Nazareth.

You can't escape your own mind. You are determined that you can bring about different results but you can't. The only result that would have any meaning would be your escape from concepts. The only thing that would possibly mean anything is your escape from the world. You can't really escape it, but by denying the world it will fade into nothing, because your determination to make it real is what is making it real. How determined are you to continue to verify your capacities as a savior in order to build a temple that verifies the separation? That is what Peter keeps asking you: What a tremendous thing you have done Lord –we've got an Academy, isn't that good? This is a demonstration of your capacity to use the establishment to bring about miraculous things for which you should be worshipped. Look how well you have afforded the student of unreality a curriculum by which he can keep his separation. That's Peter saying to Jesus don't go to Jerusalem and bring our entire aggregation there, because you will undergo a resurrection and our world will be gone. Stay with us, and let's build a temple together so that we can maintain. That's what Peter said at the transfiguration. At the transfiguration He met with the laws of man (Moses) and the prophesy of man (Elias). Peter's determination is to use the laws of man to construct himself. The meeting that Jesus had was the bringing of separation –or the laws of man, or literally the self identity containing the prophecy necessary to the self identity in the first place which would be the fulfillment of that identity –into an alignment within the continuum of time.

What did Jesus say when Peter said: let's build a temple here?"Get thee behind me, Satan." Don't stand in front of me, don't block my way. I don't want a reflection that will dim me in a memory of what I was before, which would be my establishment. Literally, get thee behind me. Jesus teaches this is all over and gone. Let it be gone. Don't seek to project the devil, Peter, the establishment in front of you. This is chapter 18 and 19 in the Course. Whole cities have arisen based on your determination to stay separate in your projected mind. Don't do that. All you'll get is the result, and the result has been to retain temporal time or separation. Don't do that and you will be home.

Miracles are real. An establishment will be an establishment, and a miracle will be a miracle. I understand that there's a relationship of cause and effect that has brought about this apparent "rock"—this apparent temple. Yet was it necessary to do that so that you could bring your aggregate of denial into the conversion necessity contained within this temple. Inevitably you will establish it very simply because you establish it. But reality is not a continuing inevitability but a single event that occurred each moment in time. It is not reached eventually. You cannot get there by the correspondence of the events of your own mind.

So there was a Healing Center that was stuck in here, a bright light of atonement, everyone came into it, and all that heard it were transformed into later time and departed. That's an occurrence in time that actually happened. Where you are in your determination to see that as an establishment that either failed or succeeded, I don't know. But the establishment neither fails nor succeeds, it transforms. Any demonstration of success in regard to the conflict will retain the conflict. You can't tell the difference between hate and pleasure and love. You release it, and it will be given you, because it is true that the miracle is all around you all the time.

This may give you something to do if we get a Healing Center. Imagine. Do you really want to test your mettle with this? The key will be to never allow the establishment to acknowledge his conceptual determination to become sick. His sickness has nothing at all to do with what he is. What he is has nothing to do with reality. Who can hear that? The way you will hear that is by the experience of the propinquity of the Center that you have established to bring that about within him. He may then go out for another million years. I am absolutely not concerned about that. I am certain that any conversion will only be the totality of what it is in that individual mind. One unreality will be exactly the same as any other unreality. One sickness is going to be exactly the same as any other sickness. The determination to correspond the cause and effect –I saw that dumb Donna from Milwaukee fight the battle of letting sin be real and attempting to combat it –we will not do that at this Center. Everyone who comes into the Center is only totally sick, which is the same as being totally sinful, if sin is separation from God. The teachings is that sickness is nothing but apparent isolation or a turning in on yourself to retain the tension of the identification of the autonomy of a space/time relationship. If you have the memory capacity of transformation contained within your own body, contained in the sense that everything is a totality of any relationship with anything. In other words, your identification of yourself as a human being is very Godly, because any identification of self-association would have to be Godly. It would have to be total unto itself, or you could not have the conflict of the totality of your own relationship –and the capacity to demonstrate it with what appears to be real within your own mind. Remember that you are using the power of Universal Mind to be or do whatever you are. You cannot *not* do that.

I don't believe that it is possible, certainly it's not possible for dumb Donna, to teach that sickness or cancer is a decision. It is a very difficult idea because it is removed from the idea of the source of the sickness, which is the mind not the body. So the sentence: "you have decided to be sick" is not of too much value. To your mind it may very well be valuable, because you are at a point in your own mind where you see that your power to decide is based on a Universal Mind that knows no conflict. That's a step you can make. At that point you can simply say: "You do not need to have cancer." There will be associations that come into your Center who can hear that. It will disappear from them immediately. I promise you this is true. They may have a revelatory experience and continue in the demonstrations of themselves. You notice I'm allowing you this these days? I'm not concerned about it. I'm going home anyway. Whatever I leave in that residual can be very valuable because the association is healed. Notice that our instruction to him is that he was not healed by any method of our association. Genuine, miraculous healing.

Now, if you blur that entirely in a conceptual identity, you'll best be able to get away with it. Don't let any doctrine of identity come into it all, and you might get away with it. You are teaching forgiveness and love. If the association is threatened by the idea that he must forgive sin, throw forgiveness out. He cannot escape the fundamental admission that pain is caused by his own mind. A great deal of progress can be made by that –throw the word *forgiveness* out. Grievance is inherent in a mind determined to suffer the conflict of its own associations. Then the solution to sickness can be seen as its capacity not to defend itself in its own associations, which will be the fundamental teaching, and certainly it can do that. There isn't anyone who will walk into your Center who will not admit that they are at least a partial cause of their own pain. The problem will be to the admission that they are the cause of their own pain in its totality, which is exactly the dilemma that you face in perceptual mind. Remember that the obstacle to peace is the necessity for the retention of the problem. I must keep the problem or the earth will disappear. I want the problem, but I don't want it solved. An amazing idea. As long as I can keep the problem, I can die in the attempt to solve it. I don't have to admit its totality.

When they walk into the Center, the first thing that you are going to tell them is: you are perfect as God created you. Any problem that you have could not possibly be a real one because God doesn't have any problems with you. If God doesn't have any problems with you, why do you want to have any problems with God? It's so simple! The reason you're laughing, that it's working, is that your mind now wants there to be a whole God, not in relationship to evil. All you really had to do is decide you wanted that to be true. How would it not be true if the cause and effect are only in your own mind? The attraction of pain cannot be that intense. It's not really an attraction of pain, it's an attraction of your capacity to overcome the pain. This is the obstacle. How would you know you're happy if you didn't have pain? Nothing to compare with! You'd have to be totally happy. If there's one thing that's intolerable to you it's being totally happy for no reason. It's the same idea as being totally healed for no reason. That's not acceptable because you'd see the earth never was in the first place –the admission of that is what salvation is.

Well, you say, I saw that for a moment back in '87 but I managed to find seven eviler associations who continued to verify me. You sought out the previous result of your mind, and you found it. What you seek, you'll find. Can you accept that you cannot *not* get the result of your own mind? You'll begin to be more careful with your thoughts. That's literally true. As you understand the power of your own mind, you will become more careful with your thoughts because you will feel the ravishes of your own pain, and you won't be able to stand it. You won't want to be angry, because you will see that the anger turns on you immediately. That's the nicest way to get it. You'll see you're doing it to yourself.

In what you call the glandular reassociations that you are demonstrating in your physiology, you may, during the process of your healing, feel incredible, passionate rage for no reason at all. If at least your rage was reasonable, you could deal with it. But what you are feeling, with the opening a channel to God, is an incredible rage –a rage in Heaven –or the demonstration of your capacity in its entirety to remain separate. Uncontrollable rage! What's the difference between uncontrollable rage and uncontrollable love? One is against and the other is for. A totality of rage against God will become Godly by the continuing reassociation of your capacity to demonstrate passion. It cannot *not*. If your rage has no focus, you will become Godly. Isn't that amazing? You need something to rage against in the correspondence of your own mind, or you will become totally evil. You can't demonstrate the totality of evil because evil is a comparison with something that is less than evil, or good. You got that? I don't...

What I want you to understand is that this is happening to you, healer of God. The certainty that the universe is one has come to you. Demonstrate that by the release of your individual necessity to find a reality where there isn't any. The process gets so simple once you recognize it. You couldn't possibly fail. Everyone who comes to your Healing Center is totally healed when he comes in the door. All he has to do is accept it. But his fear of accepting it is why he's here. This is a construct of fear of accepting the love of God. An amazing idea! He will admit to you, in many cases, I don't want to be well."I'm entitled to some pain –I can get two weeks off. I want to be sick some of the time." Life is demonstrated by the capacity to be sick. A weird place to be. God does not suffer conflict. Once you have that firmly in your mind, you will be a healer.

Once more, the dilemma: the perceptual mind, in its aggregate of its historic reference, is going to insist on placing on you a mutual correspondence with his own dream, with its own mind. Each association that will enter the Center with different formulas for the manner in which it will keep its identity, because paths do vary. But each one of them has an intention to use the power that he sees in your temple to continue to authenticate the falsity of him. He has no intention within his own conscript of reality, what he defines himself as, of undergoing the totality of an experience to the realization that he is God. His intention is exactly the opposite. Any intention to come to God with the power of your mind would immediately lead to coming to God. It could not *not*. No access is denied you, except by your own determination to deny yourself. The problem you have with it is that you think there are degrees to it. Many of you still believe that progress is being made in the association who is coming into the Healing Center. My assurance to you is that this world is not real. That certainly includes the Center where you come to get well. That being said, you would require a Center of Wholeness that you could come to in order to be well, not because it's true, but because you need a true hallucination –true in the sense that there is no conflict in regard to what you are in it, dummy, if the conflict is only in your own mind. If you are doing this but to yourself, all you would have to do is to stop doing it. This is Chapter 18.

Very simply, as a Healer of God, you are the Way and the Light, not because somebody says you are the Way and the Light, but because there is only the Way and the Light. God is the Way and God is the Light, and you are that, because you cannot *not* be! Grandiosity of your humility notwithstanding –I did that right out of the book. Jesus is very emphatic! Pride in limitation serves no purpose. Pride in limitation is the same as the authentication of method or process. This may be in preparation for the establishment of the Healing Center. I have absolutely no control over it. It's interesting that it's being controlled with the totality of the conceptual association of Jesus in *A Course In Miracles*. He really wants this. Why wouldn't He? Any demonstration of healing, in reality, is what salvation is. We have a tendency to bypass demonstration because of what I just read you. But that does not mean there is not value in miracle healing.

The result of the value of phenomena is crucifixion. It cannot *not* be because the idol must turn on you, because you have turned on yourself. This is all in the Course. But as long as the Course is here, and we are ending, literally, this gathering at the end of this package of form, the so-called residual in another timeframe will be this temple of healing that is a real temple of healing. Everything is only a facsimile of God, isn't it? Like: what's it for? What we just said is the church is to retain the conflict of separation and demonstrate limited cultural gatherings, denominations, that's what it would be. But the church of Jesus, of love, of forgiveness, is a totality that transcends through the Jonas experience the necessity of the repetition of conflict where order is evident in the grace of God.

You will be belittled for claiming no results as much as for claiming results. Remember that all belittlement is insane. It's the necessity for the defense of death. Now I'm up to the third Obstacle to Peace. Every association that walks into your temple – you, when you walked into this earth – is nothing but a determination to terminate himself and die. Your denial to that, obviously, would be a threat to him, because death is his last resort to escape from what you are teaching him. Sickness is nothing but a little death, or a verification that he can get old and die. It's an amazing idea.

You're going to say to the old guy with cancer or the young guy, or the young mother: be whole as God created you, because you are that. By the demonstration of that reality or reasonableness in the light of your mind, you can bring about –in the sense that it remains phenomenal –a healing in that association. It is brought about by the location of the demonstration of the miracle. Nothing stops that association literally from being healed in its identity, not with you, but in the certainty of your relationship with God. That's the whole teaching.

When he comes in, to his determination that you are demonstrating yourself as Jesus, he is very determined, in the first law of chaos, to keep separation valid simply by the retention of separate minds. Your teaching to him is that one separation from God will be as total as any other, and that the responsibility is his individually as the only separate association.

Are you going to be able to get this into organized Christianity? I saw Benny Hinn again. If you get a chance watch Benny Hinn. He is demonstrating healing using Holy Spirit energy, kind of like Oral Roberts when he was young. Oral Roberts' problem was not that he didn't heal, but he thought you had to have chemotherapy too. His healing contained devices by which the separation could be maintained. Our Center has no medical devices at all. In fact, it has no devices of any kind. Don't be concerned about the manner in which you are attempting to heal the association. Will it work? It works in the sense of the totality of it. It couldn't possibly fail, because all of the associations are what failure is. Yet does the mind need a demonstration of a miracle, or something beyond belief. Belief is not going to be true, this is the stuff beyond belief. Anything you believe is going to be true, including your unfaithfulness. "As a man thinketh, so he is."

Does the consciousness feel the transformation? Is that what this is, here? Are you going to teach that? I don't know. I don't know where that wants to be heard. One thing for sure, it will be heard where it wants to be. Can I get you to admit that? Any correspondence that you give is what you are going to be. When that association looked at you to see whether you were going to verify that, as though somehow your verification of it could give her an access to what we are pertaining to, has nothing to do with what I'm teaching at all. I'm just showing you how this works.

This is obviously what you are going to get in your Center. They are hell-bent not on demonstrating their mutual reality, but on demonstrating their mutual separation. They'll do anything they can to keep themselves from losing their judgment of where they are. How can you explain that? You can't. It's not explainable because the reasonableness is very apparent through the authentication of the association. Reasonableness will always be an assertion of a result based on a need within your own mind, and it will seem reasonable. But coming to God does not seem reasonable to perceptual mind, and that is why faith is required, because the idea of wholeness is not reasonable to perception, since perception is the reasonability of an unreasoning God. Obviously, separation could not serve a purpose except to stay separate, and the outcome of that separation could only be time or death, or loss of life. But life is eternal. So it's impossible to lose life. Therefore, anything that you lose was never lost. This is not life. Is this life? Am I alive?

Of course I failed, how could I succeed? That's the whole teaching. You're so happy that you couldn't succeed at this. If you could have succeeded, you'd have to stay in friction forever. You have built in death in order to fail, because you couldn't stand the conflict of your need to stay separate.

Have you ever seen a widow curse her husband because he died to get out of the responsibility? Into this impossible situation you find yourself. It is not possible that the whole mind, the Universal Mind, be in conflict with anything because it simply is everything. It has nothing to do with whether you think it's in conflict. Can there be harmony in conflict? That's what love is. That's what forgiveness is. Perception requires an alignment or act of love, because God is a totality of action, not a static condition of potential identity. Use up your possibilities, then the totality of what you are will emerge. Everything must be true by the possibility of it, and certainly your return to Heaven would be a part of that. Are you ready: you never really left.

There's a tremendous amount or correspondence, or communication, going on. What is your Center? We could even call it a Communication Center. Years ago I might have been able to recognize it as a Communication Center. This is an access to Universal Mind. Healing Centers are nothing but Communication Centers since the definition of time is a break in communication, a momentary loss of communication. What is the vehicle that you use? Prayer. You'd have to because the power is in your own mind. That's not the problem. The problem is: do you want the schism healed? Do you want this to be over? Are you going to teach it?

When an association comes in you say: do you really want to be perfect as God created you. He'll say: of course I do. Then you say: Well, you are! He'll say: how is that so? And you'll say: what the hell difference does it make? It's a miracle. It's going to be true because it is true. It can be taught because it's become lucid to you. There is a sufficiency of light within your own mind to extend from you a correspondence of unity that will be reflected back to you because there is nothing outside of you. What's hard to teach is that you pass through the darkness of your light if the darkness doesn't hear you, or you'll get a reflection of your old correspondence. It's the reverse of what you think. If I don't allow this to obstruct me in my own mind identity, I will literally look right through it, in the sense that looking is reasonable and my own creative mind needs a reasonableness to be demonstrated by the manner in which my mind reasons.

What we're saying is that singularity is reasonable to you. That's very difficult. The process of reason is not what singularity is. Reason certainly can be used, because it's an empowerment of the totality of mind. You can literally see reason. There's no reason why you can't be as God created you. What would the reason be if God is what everything is. That seems reasonable. You didn't get any result for it. As soon as it seems reasonable to you, you got the result. The demonstration of the result is what has kept you in your unreasonableness. What you are saying is: there is no reason for the world. It has no cause. Being causeless, it does not exist. Sounds like *A Course In Miracles.*

We need to broaden the range of revelation and de-doctrinize it in the cultural establishment. We'll do it within the Christian vernacular because we're in the Christian vernacular. Obviously, our concern is not with healing, healing is what God is. He who heals has nothing to do with it. Just as certainly, if your faith is in idols, you will get the idolatry of that association, it will become a God to you, so you can subsequently judge it as inadequate because of your own inadequacies –condemn it or crucify it through a reassociation of what you are determined to be –rather than simply admitting that your brother is your savior. The only thing I can positively guarantee you is that your brother is your savior very simply because your brother is you. You are the savior of yourself in the totality of the realization that you are perfect as God created you. Do you believe me? He that believeth unto me, unto this message, unto what I am as a savior, will never die.

You included yourself in with yourself and were found not guilty. There is no such thing as yourself."My revelation has left me in a place where there isn't anything." This is the moment... This is chapter 19. Stand there a moment and shut up. You immediately seek somewhere in there for a verification of yourself. This is the moment you've been most afraid of. You've lost all your establishments, you've either given them away, or they left you or something, you frantically better seek some more. Or how else are you going to be sick? How else are you going to be a body? How else are you going to retain the animosity of this little place that you find yourself in. You must demonstrate your capacity to get old and sick. After all, everything here gets old and sick. You're a joke.

I never can understand this Healing Center. You'll look the association in the eye and not be able to understand why he could possibly want to be what he maintains he is. Yet his determination of maintenance is what his own death is. By maintaining himself, he verifies its own reality through death?"You're telling me not to maintain myself at all." I'm not telling you not to maintain yourself. I'm telling you to maintain yourself totally. The establishment will maintain that you are teaching no maintenance in a comparison with God, which is a form of maintenance. I want you to understand this. The Center is going to come real fast. If you stay out of the specific reference of the association, you will never be bound to the relationship of cause and effect. If somebody says to you: "I've come to your Center and I have a headache." What do you say to him?"Take an aspirin." You don't say: "don't take an aspirin, will your headache away." Using what: non-headache power? Don't get trapped in this. They'll trap you if they can. The best way is to put it completely out in the open. Then it just gets foolish. They don't know what to attack. It's too outrageous. That's another way to not believe what the Course says, deny that it says it. Absurd. *A Course In Miracles* is a course in remembering that you are Universal Mind and perfect as God created you. Do you have a problem with that? Certainly not with what it says. You may have a problem in your own admission of it, but you have no problem that it says that.

If you set up a Center of healing, you're not concerned about the perception's denial of what you are teaching, you are only concerned that they understand what you are teaching within the concept of what they deny: that the world is a denial of God. That's reasonable. Nothing is accomplished by war. But you already know that. What could be accomplished by war but another form of war or separation? Don't make war and you'll be in Heaven.

Need the association be concerned at your Center about other aspects of its relationship? There is no answer to that because he is a condition of concern about his own relationship. That's what miraculous healing is —it is a loss of concern about anything that is not directed to the totality of his new relationship with God. At that point there is a certain vigilance that will apply. But that faith is individual. We are not setting up examples of faith. Faith cannot be demonstrated except in unfaithfulness. Faithfulness is a momentary complete reassociation of the demonstration of the totality of conceptual mind. It's an innate thing in your capacity to be as God created you, not by the demonstration of your antecedinal thoughts. Everything is going to be whole, no matter what you do. Understand?

Will there be Biblical references at the Healing Center? Yes. One of the big ones will be: "Be ye perfect even as your Father in Heaven is perfect." We are not quarreling about the doctrine of Jesus, but simply allowing for his simple declarations of uncompromising reassociations to be what they are. How much difficulty will we have with that? Your mindful conceptual associations aren't as conflictual as they used to be.

Healing is nothing but the loss of the continuing contraptual evidence of your demonstration of your own separation, and the admission that one condition is the same as any other, or your incapacity to deal with separate situations and having them reoccurring, is the admission of the power of God-mind, or whole Universal Mind. Yet, that ability to do that is an action of what you would call a contraption of motivational effort contained within the apparent conceptual reality. It's very important that you understand that I know your mind is a mechanism. It cannot not be so because you live in objective reality where there is a mechanism involved.

What you must finally see is I am not concerned with the fact that your mind is a mechanism. It is finally a mechanism of decision. All I'm trying to show it is that within its decision-making possibilities must be a totality of mind, very simply because any decision is a capacity to see yourself as whole or no decision could be made.

There is no question you will get the result of your own identity within your own mind. You're getting that –we're doing that right now. That result will lead to another result and will lead to a correspondence of results in the perceptual mind. You are a correspondence, then, of results of your mind form. You hold that together in association with what you are. Who are you? I am the result of the correspondence of my own mind.

They just had a new quantum physicist maintain that since they now have duplicated what the universe was like one billionth of a second after the Big Bang, that quantum now proves that before the Big Bang there was nothing. Subsequently we came from nothing. Is that true? It's not reasonable. Unless I am nothing. Which is exactly what the quantum physicist maintains. Why does he maintain that? He's now arrived at a conclusion of the futility of any process. He's within a billionth of a second. He's getting closer and closer. What an amazing idea. He's trying to fit himself into the breakage point. Do you see that? It's like a piece has been broken out of the whole. He identifies himself to the piece and is trying to fit himself into it. He just keeps getting closer and closer and closer. If I see myself as broken, I cannot come home. You cannot find union in separation. If there is objective reality, there could not be total subjectivity. Objects indicate separation of mind, and separation of thought.

Obviously the human condition is fearful; that's what it is. Your identity that you maintain is a maintenance of your capacity to be a body and to be what you are. That's what you do. That's what you are. Can you successfully do that? Yes. You're doing it right now. You're going to maintain that you are what you are not. Boy are you good at it. A whole world has emerged that is going to verify your necessity to be a body to get sick and die. If you are in a condition of atonement, you will not understand the conceptual mind. Why not? Because it is not understandable. No matter how much he tries to explain himself to you, you're finally going to admit that he cannot be understood. You don't know who you are or how you got here, but you're determined to demonstrate that you do. I do not understand that. Will you explain that to me, please? The whole world is nothing but your attempt to explain who you are to an association that you believe is separate from you. None of that is real.

So objectivity is nothing but living in the center of previous thoughts verified in form and shooting off of that potential within your own limitation, and sharing the limitation together. Yet the minds can never join –how could they? They apparently have separate sources of reality. If we have a common source, where is our conflict?

Obviously there is a problem or you wouldn't need the atonement. Just as obviously the statement: "here is a whole, loving Universal Mind creating forever" must be a true statement. Why? You said so. How do you know about it? Now, where's the conflict? Well, everywhere I look, I find a need to identify myself and assert myself as what I am. All I'm telling you is that it is non-communicative. There's a whole universe out there that you are not seeing because of your limited perspective of what you are. Yet your fear is of the expansion of your own conceptual association with yourself because it will be a loss of the old association you had with yourself. It's the teaching of you've got nothing to lose. If you lose it, it would be nothing anyway. There is no loss. If I have nothing to lose by going with God, I'm better able to give up the world. My value system isn't going to work anyway. Was that only in your mind? Is there really only one mind separate? Sure. You need be what you are because need is what you are –the necessity for the maintenance of you. It is a statement of itself. Having thoughts is the problem. I've taught you to see the pain that you're in.

Don't put off the inevitable. What's the inevitable? Eternal life! You thought it was death.

I certainly hope I'm right about this. The more you hope I'm right about it, the more I'll be right about it. None of your retention of yourself will hold up if you bring them to the light. It's your intense final fear to bring them to the light, because you'll have to admit I'm right about this, and that you are perfect as God created you, and never left your home, and you don't want to do that. Now we're at the page where it says: go call on some more of your buddies. I watch you do it. And they're going to tell you that you're OK., and implore you not to go off the deep end: "stay here with us. Look how attractive we are. Don't tell me my cancer is not real." This is your whole Healing Center. We're not telling them their cancer is not real, we're telling them *they* are not real. The discovery that someone is causing their own cancer is an amazing thing. It can only be done by a whole mind. That's what healing is. It has no concern about what's being healed at all. The practice of that at the Healing Center will be the term: "shame on you for letting your brother be sick." You have associations in your own mind that you say: I can't do anything about that, he's determined to be sick. That's not true. You see them as whole in your mind, and do not allow for the contingency of your association, and they will be whole. What you don't want to accept is your own atonement. It would be impossible that they're not healed if you are healed, because you literally cannot see their sickness. All you could possibly see is your own reflection of yourself."We're all working on this together." Nonsense. There are no others. All establishments are to death!

There is no such thing as a human being. I'm not a human being. You can be one if you want to, but you'll be the only one, and you won't be real. What an assemblage of nothing! It's absurd. It's what hell is. You see a beautiful body and it rots in front of your eyes. So you withdraw from the world, and contemplate your situation. Vanity, vanity, all is vanity. That doesn't solve the problem, it just looks at it. Do you mean if I change my mind, the whole world will change? You're so afraid of the power of your mind that you can't stand it.

I wouldn't be telling you this if it wasn't true. What possible reason would I have standing here and telling you this if it wasn't true? You are so suspicious that you can't stand yourself. I'm only standing here telling you that you are perfect and whole as God created you. What would I gain? There is nothing to gain here. All I could gain is death. You think I'm trying to get something from you. . The last thing I would want is what you have. You say: you can't take this from me. Why would I want it? My freedom is in giving everything away. What's going to amaze you at the Healing Center is that you are a threat. Your healing is going to be a threat. All I'm saying is there is a Universal Mind, and you are a part of that. There is no conflict, there is only one thing. And it's you.

The most interesting thing is that as long as you can maintain dual saviorships you feel secure because you can maintain that there are attributes and qualities in me that will avail someone, and not you. When I say that I am your personal savior, I mean that literally. I know that you will persist in saying that I'm teaching that you are all saviors. I'm not teaching that at all. I'm teaching there is no such thing as saviorship, and most emphatically what you think I am. Any designation you have of me is designed to keep you dead. Why else are you here? If I am anything in your mind, I am your savior and the savior of the world. Can you differentiate in your mind between people? I just tried to tell you apart and I couldn't. You think I should be able to tell the difference. I'm sorry I can't do it. What would the difference be if it is perfect? I don't need explanations, I need transformation. One thing for sure, if we are different, you are condemned to a different association based on what you think you are. That way you can be secure because you can compare us without admitting who is doing the comparison. You can really subtract yourself and then you can live in the comparison of your own projected associations based on your capacity to tell this association from this one, which is what you are. Can you see that? Why would you want there to be a difference?

So you can tell the difference. If you couldn't tell the difference, you might mistake me for her. You might go home tonight and get in bed with a complete stranger. If you don't find yourself in a strange place, you'll always be in Heaven."You're forcing me to admit that we're all the same." Bullshit. I'm telling you that we're all completely different. You keep trying to establish reality.

CHAPTER FIVE

Physical Resurrection

Christians: I'm going to talk about physical resurrection for a minute. I'm waiting for the spirit. The spirit is always there, but sometimes you keep making decisions... Sometimes when you're trying to express something that has occurred to you, it's difficult.

Obviously Saul-became-Paul is going to have a problem explaining to the world why he is completely different than he was just a minute ago. He is going to have a problem doing that. Here he is attacking the Christians and doing everything he can. He's very determined in his own mind to wipe them out, and suddenly he's knocked off his horse and the Voice says "why are you doing that?" He undergoes this monstrous physical conversion which includes that he was blind and he was nursed back to health and he is an entirely different man, and I am going to use the term *man* here for a minute –because obviously he's still a man. But just as obviously he's entirely different than he was a minute ago.

There is no one in this Christian church who does not understand somewhere within the nature of him that this is what Christianity is. Christianity is nothing but a conversion of the mind of the cause and effect relationship –that is what you would call an eye for an eye –to the certainty that God is love, brought about by a conversion or a transformation of the mind.

This is Bible class. Is there anyone who disagrees that this is what Christianity is? The question is not that, the question involves two things: If you are speaking of the resurrection of Jesus of Nazareth through the perfection of His mind, a man, in association with the certainty of the creation of God, at what point in your relationship with yourself are you able to identify with Jesus of Nazareth? If indeed, Jesus of Nazareth is the savior of the world, and if indeed Jesus of Nazareth experienced a body awakening, a body transformation, a body resurrection, at what point will He call to me as a body resurrected and say "here I am, not dead, come on home with me!"

This is where the difficulty arises. This is not at all different from Corinthians 15, and I'm going to read it to you for just a minute. Paul says, "don't you all remember when He was here?" There is an assumption in a physical letter written by Paul to the Corinthians that all of them know that Jesus resurrected. That's an astonishing thing, isn't it? You're teaching physical resurrection.

Let's look at it: This is about 55 AD, presuming that Jesus resurrected in about 33 AD This is about 20 years after the resurrection. And obviously Jesus, after the resurrection, appeared in physical form, not that it did any good. But there is no question that Jesus arose physically. Let's read: Moreover, brethren, I declare unto you the gospel which I preached unto you, which also ye have received, and wherein ye stand; by which also ye are saved, if ye keep in memory what I preached unto you, unless ye have believed in vain. For I delivered unto you first of all that which I also received, how that Christ died for our sins according to the scriptures; and that He was buried, and that He rose again the third day according to the scriptures. This is nothing but Paul saying that this is what we all know. Now he's going to say something like: you were His original disciples, I was His last disciple because He was obviously already gone when He got to me but there is no question that He appeared to me and told me precisely this.... and that he was seen of Cephas, then of the twelve. After that he was seen of above 500 brethren at once; of whom the greater part remain unto this present, but some are fallen asleep. (I Cor 15:1-6)

The fact of the matter is that those who were still alive, had seen Him risen, were Christians. There's no question about that because Paul had to remind them: don't you remember you saw Him dead and then three days later He began to appear all around the countryside?

He was physically in His body teaching. Not only that but He would appear behind closed doors. He was capable of suddenly appearing in flesh. His first appearance was behind closed doors. He wasn't used to walking around yet. He did what is called a temporal reoccurrence rather than a spatial one.

Part of the problem in the resurrection is the association of space/time. I'm going to cover it from *A Course In Miracles* for a minute: First of all we need the admission that He was appearing physically before the people who had known Him –or hadn't known Him. He obviously had more effect on the people who had known Him because they knew He was dead. He had less and less effect on people who did not know Him –99. 9% of the world, who was totally disinterested in Him to begin with. They couldn't care less. They were not concerned about His resurrection simply because they had never heard of Him and didn't know what He was.

But we are still talking of physical resurrection: After that He was seen of James, (His brother), then of all the apostles, and last of all he was seen of me also, as of one born out of due time. For I am the least of the apostles, that am not meet to be called an apostle, because I persecuted the church of God. But by the grace of God I am what I am; and His grace which was bestowed upon me was not in vain. (I Cor 15:7-10) I don't know how it happened to me, but I've got a job to do! I don't know what I did to God that caused Him to forgive me, but I've got a job to teach the resurrection. I know that. This sounds very familiar to me. Not coming from what you would call a Christian tradition, all of a sudden I'm struck with God. So converts are always more fervent than those who think they already know. Converts come from a place of not knowing, through the grace of God, to a place of knowing. They are more liable to be more fervent in the declaration of what they received. Why? Experience! The experience was required for them to get it.

... yet not I, but the grace of God which was with me. Therefore, whether it were I or they, so we preach, and so ye believed. Now if Christ be preached that he rose from the dead, how say some among you that there is no resurrection of the dead? (I Cor 15:11-12) They're already beginning to do it.

We're dealing with physical resurrection. Here's Paul saying: remember this man rose, physically. And their answer was: What good does that do me? What good does the phenomenon of the resurrection of the physical body do me? The answer to that is: it does you total good if you will let the phenomenon, the miracle of the occurrence, be true in the association with yourself in regard to the transformation of the existent perceptual identity of yourself in regard to the phenomenon that is occurring. That is true because the energetic determination of a resurrecting body contains the Christ of universal mind.

If Jesus walked into this room today, He obviously would not be recognized by most of the corresponding associations in the world. They would not recognize Him because He, from their definition, at best, in His physical resurrection would be a containment of a temporal reassociation of Himself as a phenomenon rising to Heaven. I'll demonstrate it. I'll rise off the ground –shall I do that for you? –and I'll go right through the roof and I'll be gone. I was going to read that to you. That's in Acts 1:1. So He rises up and everybody stands there and watches Him as He ascends and there they sit in their bodies.

Here's the way we are teaching this today: The temporal reference of the conversion of the body, the resurrection of your individual physical body, is the declaration of the certainty that you, as son of man, are also son of God and that conversion occurs in the temporal association. This gets into quantum physics. What I want you to see is that at no single moment –I'm talking time here now –if at no single moment the body is real, in a particular sense it is always undergoing a resurrection. Is this so? Are you comfortable with this? Now that resurrection could well be demonstrated, and will be —those of you who have watched me rise—there is no big deal about rising off the ground, why would that be such a big deal? It might impress you that there's some funny guy out there that can rise off the ground. One thing for sure: if it's a phenomenon to you, you must call it to your attention in a way that you can understand it. So while it may be miraculous, if it is within your range of understanding, it will be a magical denial of the occurrence. It would have to be. A week from now, you'll say I did it with mirrors. Two weeks from now, you'll say it was a trick to get you to admit that I...

You see, there is no manner in which you can come to know it in the temporal association with me very simply because if you know it in the temporal association with me, you will be resurrected. Healers! Healers: You will be resurrected by the temporal moment of Jesus rising up.

There is no question of the rising up –the ascension seen by 500. Now here was the guy that they had never seen and he says: why is everyone around him? I'm going to try to explain it to the guy who just walked up. He says: why is everyone standing on the hill listening to this guy talk? And you say: You should have heard what happened two weeks ago. He was dead. We all saw him die, we saw the nails, we saw him bleed and we saw him laid in the tomb and now he's risen. And the guy says, wow, that's amazing. Now it's become nothing but a story of the physical association of the resurrection of a body, and it's been that for 2,000 years. The strange part about it is that when any association in the demand to know God –this has happened thousands, millions of times in the last 2,000 years –where individual associations have experienced the Light of universal mind and have felt the peace of God and have been transcended in their associations, any attempts to explain it or demonstrate it must become phenomenal. They immediately become difficult because the conceptual mind –I'll teach *A Course In Miracles* for a moment –is limited in its temporal associations with itself to a spatial projection of its mind. It cannot go beyond what has been converted in its own body-mind. This is Paul, too: natural man is in a natural body and he will see natural things from his temporal association to his spatial identity. It's interesting to see what actually occurs –as your individual atonement, healing, transfiguration, physical resurrection of your body occurs –in relationship with the spatial evidence of the separation of your cause and effect. Letting the causation be your time and the effect be your space, they can be reversed.

So here you are as a resurrecting body, but without a holy association, without a place, all you will do is to continue to occur among the phenomena and disappear. If what we are teaching is true, you, as an entity of consciousness, physically in space/time, are endowed with the Christ, or the capacity to resurrect instantly. **In actuality you are continually resurrecting.** This would have to be so very simply because the resurrection is the absence, or loss of time and space actually, in the moment that occurs. But the resurrection, then in time, requires a demonstration of space —or it simply would not be. If you simply came here and resurrected, you would be gone. So space is the second day, that's the day you came in here. Now, the place where you resurrect is holy in the sense that it remains temporal. This is the provision for holiness in correspondence with cause and effect relationships. So here we are, now, faced with a phenomenon of temporal or physical resurrection that is going on in your body, and I'm going to go to you as Jesus would teach it: greater things will you do than I have done. This is all nothing but Jesus of Nazareth. He says to you: my body underwent a physical resurrection. Your body can also undergo a physical resurrection and you will be whole in Heaven with me.

Notice that the demonstration or the continuation of the message of Jesus did not occur with those who saw Him rise physically. Instead it occurred with those who saw Him rise spatially, or the utilization of the energy of His physical resurrection demonstrated, say at Damascus (Paul's conversion), or more particularly if I were to do Acts 2, Pentecost. If you move from the continuation of the physical resurrection of Jesus or the conversion of His body to Light to what you call a unified field of energy, this is precisely what the requirement of Pentecost is. The difficulty that the human conceptual associations have with this is that to an awakened mind there is no difference in space and time.

To me, I can appear here physically and eat fish behind closed doors and be very much aware that I am an integration of the Holy Spirit or the unifying field that is all about me and this is what's happening to you. Say "Amen."

I began to experience the temporal reassociation of my body. That's a miracle. The interesting part about it is that a miracle just happened here by your acceptance, not of my spirit, but initially of my physical appearance, without the necessity to judge who I was in your frame of reference. Because if you judge who I was in your frame of reference, a temporal resurrection won't mean anything to you. It can't because you already defined me as a human being!

Obviously, you're not defining me, you're forgiving me by your own definition of yourself and are allowing the spatial miracle to occur. Will that heal? Of course it will heal. Why? There's really only one body. Bodies aren't really separate. It's just your body converting. (I'm trying to stay out of that and stay with this for a minute.) I almost went through the resurrection!

Jesus says you must accept atonement for yourself. You are a continuing temporal reassociation that locates it somewhere and believes that he's in an objective association of space/time. Not only that but he believes the body that he is involved with is a validation of that space/time. Jesus says very simply on the mount, and Paul says it –your body is not real because this place is not real. This is a particular way to look at it, since it is going to require the conversion of your own body to make the place real. As long as you believe you can convert the place, you'll be trapped in a space/time location. The place is an effect of your own mind, but you don't know that. So you keep trying to make places holy. Let every place be holy and you will temporally, in your own experience, make it a space/time relationship.

It's nothing but the teachings of Paul or Jesus. He says that natural man cannot possibly know of spiritual man, can he? He's not in the same time frame. He can be in the same space frame, but he's not in the same time frame. So when New Man enters into a new time frame, he also enters into a new space frame. Why? Space/time is always going on all the time anyway. So the reason you will find that you can't communicate with human beings is not because you are not in what you might even think, or what he is allowing you to think is the same space, but you are literally in a different time. That's true. If you want to look at that as an acceleration of the correspondence of your own association –that is you are undergoing a resurrection more rapidly than he is. It's going to take him 8,000 years to resurrect. Quite literally, he has to do it, he's just in a slower frame of reference in correspondence with his location. As long as he can determine his location based on his old references he can retain himself trapped in his cause and effect of space time. Never mind what Einstein tells you. Never mind what any association tells you. That's relative and going on in you.

Wherever you are in your spatial/temporal associations it might be nice for you to remember that the universe is ideas and that all of the thoughts that have ever been had by any human being in any what you call spatial/temporal hallucination or realization of particle identity or memories is still with us. And it is also true that there are locations, acupuncture points of the world, where there is more energy in reassociation with Jesus. This is why people go to Jerusalem or Mecca or wherever they go to feel the energy of the reassociation. Not only is that true, but holy spirit—integrating fields of energy—this is all late stuff: if it is true in time, it would also be true in space. It's hard to teach that, but space and time are actually the same. What Jesus says about this in the Bible and Paul says, when you undergo a temporal reassociation of the correspondence of yourself, you affect everything else in all of space as well as time. That's the latest teaching going on. What that will amount to, if you continue in that idea, is that every human being is actually in a totality of a spatial/temporal reference of single identity. The memories of the conversion of your mind will affect all of the associations who correspond to you spatially. They've had big tests now to prove that is absolutely true. We are what you would call ontological associations. There is a fundamental admission in all of us that we are using the power of God-mind with which to organize spatial/temporal associations. The demonstration of that is what is known as a miracle or the phenomenon of the healing association despite what the correspondence appears to be in space/time. At that moment it is a uniting of space/time reference. It would have to be. How else could you correspond with the association?

Certainly the salvation of the world depends on you initially as the Christ. As Jesus would say: "Greater things will you do than I have done." He will stand right here. I'll try it: I'm standing right here in front of you in a physical body telling you I'm not here. That's exactly what He says. I died. And I am gone to Heaven. That is literally a statement. The demonstration of that would have to be the continuing transformation of my body association. When Paul tries to explain it he says: I just keep on dying all the time. The whole *Course In Miracles* says nothing but keep on dying all the time. Don't hold on to your own reference and you will undergo the resurrection. Why is that so fearful? Two reasons: It's a loss of time and a loss of space. If you are in the rigidity of time within your own body, in a cause and effect relationship of past and future references, how could you find a holy spot if the holy spot is where you are standing? The holy instant, then is actually a spot of innocence. The holy instant is actually a spot where you are actually standing. And I mean that is a holy place. You are in a holy place. Admit to the holiness of your relationship and your place must become holy very simply –this is the first 50 lessons of the Workbook of *A Course in Miracles* –because God is everywhere. Therefore everywhere that you are is holy.

Could I teach this in a regular Christian church? Or would they be yelling at me: how dare you tell me I'm perfect as God created me? The heretics are really excited. Those who have been burned for saying this are very excited at the possibility that you might let Jesus into the Christian establishment. You can't let Jesus into the Christian establishment without converting it. The establishment is a location designed to stay in time and doesn't dare experience the transformation of your resurrecting body. It's got to kick you out of the church, which is the same as crucifying you.

So, everywhere you go as a teacher of God, this is what Jesus asked you to do, you seem to be trapped in your own historic reference here. There is no question that Jesus was a man. I can read you this. And there's no question that you saw Him resurrect. And there's no question that if you come into any temporal association that will verify that you could see Him resurrect now. But by seeing Him resurrect now, you would remain in your own temporal association. This is the second coming. I'm back to tell you I never really left. When I come back in my entirety, it will be time for your resurrection as the entire you. Otherwise you will continue operating under a transformation of the spatial association without the total conversion of your temporal identity. That is, if I walked into the tavern where the Pentecost occurred. This is very soon after Jesus has actually physically ascended. And they're gathered together and they're telling the stories about this phenomenon. Actually they're outside the Jewish community. There are a lot of other associations that when He appeared as body, were testified to by His disciples that they had witnessed it. So they came together and surer than heck there occurred a spatial anomaly. Not a temporal anomaly, but a spatial anomaly.

Let's read what happens when this earthquake suddenly occurs. This did not have to do with the individual associations in their correspondence with themselves, because they were not yet perfected in their temporal identities. This occurred in the congregation of the entirety of the spatial/temporal reference. In Acts he describes: Ye men of Galilee, why stand ye gazing up into Heaven? this same Jesus, which is taken up from you... (Acts 1:11) This is the Spirit speaking to them. Acts actually describes Jesus rising up. And the voice says why are you staring up at him, dummies?! A voice from Heaven says that: Ye shall receive power, after that the Holy Spirit is come upon you; and ye shall be witnesses unto me both in Jerusalem, and in all Judea, and in Samaria, and unto the uttermost part of the earth. (Acts 1:8) So surer than heck in Acts 2, Pentecost occurs: And when the day of Pentecost was fully come, they are all with one accord in one place. (Acts 2:1) This is the idea that if you come together with one intent perceptually that spatial associations will work regardless of your temporal misnomers. That is, no matter what you may believe about your own association, if you'll come together –this is what you'll be as a teacher of God. Hopefully there will be enough allowance for you, so that when they come in, this is what Jesus calls a little willingness, that if they'll come in, at the very minimum, they will experience the phenomenon of occurrence of Holy Spirit.

This is what the Healing Center is for. They may not be entirely converted in their temporal associations. That through the act of repentance, or "I can't do it," they will experience an integration of the Holy Spirit that will heal their body and raise their minds correspondingly in a spatial/time relationship to literally a different spatial/temporal place. Is that so? Is that what you're trying to do over there in the Dells? What you're actually saying is, if you look at the continuum, that you will draw a circle around that place, or better it's a square between somewhere out there –a geographical square. The associations that enter into that will begin to have spiritual experiences, spatial spiritual experiences, that affect their temporal identities with themselves. Is this so? That's true.

Use the restaurant or the church here: we are giving welcome to temporal identities that are not in our temporal association. You are coming together in love and forgiveness and offering the association, through the transformation of your mind, a unity –first of an integration of the love of God and then to a purpose for which there would be a reason for the association to be here at all. Certainly any reason for the association to be here would have to be to undergo the experience that you are attempting to share with him. You are not natural man anymore, you have become very spiritual. Astonishingly enough, and natural man cannot understand this, the more you integrate the association into the spatial identity, the more determined you are to be spiritual rather than human. That's simply the fact of the matter. They'll say: "yeah, but why don't you go to work and worship God on Sunday." And you say: "no, I do that all the time." All Paul says is "be with me all the time." Because if you are with me all the time, you will create a spatial reference that will literally transform the physical association. It's all an illusion anyway. It's all a projection of your own mind. And here you are coming together with new projections later on in time that can integrate into the harmony of the great ray associations. Say AMEN.

The amazing part of it is that I really don't care if you're agreeing with me spatially or temporally. What do I care? One will convert to the other if you don't hold it together. I'm teaching *A Course In Miracles*. You can deny me spatially or you can deny me temporally. Obviously, if you deny me spatially, you're still going to have to have your own temporal experience. Now if you'll admit to me spatially, it will accelerate your temporal experience with yourself. It cannot not because you and I are actually perfectly created by God. There is no difference in our minds at the level of our recognition, only at the level of our denial.

Why do I have so much energy in denial? I have no intention of denying anything. What did I do? I entered into the moment of my spatial fear. I let myself become spatially fearful and I immediately resurrected. YES!! What the temporal-ness does is avoid the spatial moment of fear. The whole *Course in Miracles* –Jesus will say "I didn't come to offer you the peace, I came to offer turmoil. I came to stir you up in your own association with yourself." Where is the holiest moment? At the most chaotic!

I did what you would call an astral conversion of the Square in Amsterdam. I've never seen animosity like it. This doesn't have to do with the occurrence. It has to do with my energy. I was asked to do a repair where the Dutch Freedom Fighters were cut down by the Nazis after the War had ended. To the human condition, they don't mind war, but there has to be justice involved in it. And there couldn't be anything less just than when the Freedom Fighters, after the War was officially over, came out to celebrate and they were mowed down. I'm not concerned with the occurrence, there are no sides in regard to this, but this is a place of intense animosity where there was an attempt to form a neutrality so that the association could forgive the practice of the attack on himself –of course he doesn't know that. There's no other way that could occur. What I did was give them a brighter frame of reference if they want to use it. It became very noticeable, there was a lot of phenomena in the square, the lights came on and all sorts of nice stuff. How does that affect you directly? Not at all. Except if you would like to look at the idea that the furies are around you all the time. And that you protect yourself from your own fear of your own cellular memory and thereby retain the grievance of your determination to condemn your brother in association with your own mind. You are always meeting at the grievance of that point, where you remember that. How would you not hold, then, the animosity at that point? It is through your forgiveness that the conversion of that occurs.

So here they are, all gathered together in Pentecost: And suddenly there came a sound from Heaven as of a rushing mighty wind, and it filled all the house where they were sitting. And there appeared unto them cloven tongues like as of fire, and it sat upon each of them. And they were all filled with the Holy Ghost, and began to speak with other tongues, as the Spirit gave them utterance. And there were dwelling at Jerusalem Jews, devout men, out of every nation under Heaven. Now when this was noised abroad, the multitude came together, and were confounded, because that every man heard them speak in his own language. (Acts 2:2-6) Nice phenomenal idea there that minds communicate, bodies don't. When that occurs, that's an evidence of a healing, when you don't attempt to separate me by the language of your conceptual identity. You experience the joy and the harmony of our reassociation.

So the Bible class for today is that the phenomenon of physical resurrection requires the correspondence of the Spirit, or all the associations will do here is study the dead tomb. That's where you want to assume your role as teacher of the Course. Obviously you find yourself here with associations that are studying the dead tomb. That is, "He was here, but He is no longer here." You are trapped with the admission of the physical resurrection of Jesus of Nazareth. It is impossible for that not to turn into an objective spatial/temporal association which you will call a church, with the idolization of that association and the necessity for an intermediary to define and express the occurrence. That's called a church. What that says is: let me describe to you what happened during Jesus' resurrection. I have a better knowledge of it than you do, and can teach you how that can come about using the forgiveness technique of Jesus, but with the fundamental admission of the necessity that sin be real. All Jesus ever really said is: Sin Is Not Real. All priesthoods say is: Jesus, who was sinful, became whole. All Jesus said is: I Was Never Sinful. This is obviously the dilemma in which you find yourself now.

It's interesting that the gathering going on in Amsterdam, which is really starting to spread now, is nothing but your converting temporal associations. It appears to be separate spatially, in ranges of conflict of association, that is particles, that as they begin to draw the circle of Light will manifest a continuum, a stratum, of space/time, that is extremely harmonious. Why shouldn't it? We're all using the same energy anyway. Just as obviously, your admission of transformation would be required for you to participate in the late-time association. Otherwise, all of your correspondences will continue to die in the reference you have of yourself. How could they not? They're products of your own mind. This is *A Course In Miracles*: Behold, brother, at your hands I die.

Quite literally, wherever we are in our temporal references, we have established a spatial reference that denies our Godhood and our mutual admission that we come from a common source. Contained within that spatial reference must be what appears to be a termination of the temporal identity, very definitively because the temporal identity is holding itself in a friction of a correspondence of the location and the place it's in. Jesus teaches this in the Course by saying: you really think you came here and the world was waiting for you to make an imprint on it. That's not true. What he says very directly is that you brought this world with you when you came.

The reassociations now are of a far greater magnitude than was manifest 2,000 years ago. Not in what you would call the relative demonstration, but in the totality of the reassociation. I'm giving you that as a fact. I'm standing here and you are evolving to the fact of my mind. Everyone must come to know that there is no world. I am resurrected. This is all Jesus ever said. And He said it to a dead one here as much as he said it to a live one. Where they are going to be in their own association must determine where they are. How else can you know? It's being determined by your own mind. Your defenses against your own perfection cannot prevail because you are perfect. No matter how demanding you are, you can get old and sick and die in your temporal associations, but He Is Risen. And He Is Risen must be you because there is only one mind.

I have no problem in the admission that there is a Risen Son of God at all. If you have a problem, the problem is contained within your own mind. That must be so because the world is over. Whether you're going to be able to walk into churches and say: behold, my kingdom is not of this world, and neither is yours, I don't know. It appears to be time for it. Yet is that time determined by your converted spatial reference in correspondence with the occurrence of your own conversion of body. That's from the Holy Bible.

At first your reformation will be viewed as political. That is you're going to express yourself as: I'm going to go directly to God. You have formulated a form of Protest-ism which says: I do not need an intermediate to correspond with God. But you cannot have what you call Protest-ism, what you call Lutheranism, without it going to Calvinism. The evolution of Calvinism is the admission that God is and that man has nothing to do with it. Lutheranism says that you gain salvation through the grace. But unless God sets terms for salvation which is predestination or Calvinism, everybody could be forgiven. If that's true, let people sell the indulgences and at the last moment – you can be as wicked as you want – and when you're about to die you can say "forgive me" and you're forgiven. Obviously that's not going to be tolerable. Calvin says very simply that won't work, but since God knows about this there must be a predestination where the outcome of the saved ones will be determined and the sinners are condemned to hell forever. That's the way it would have to work.

Guys, it's all the slaughter of the innocent. Servetus, the great Spanish mystic who was a great physician, worked with the circulation of the blood and worked on cadavers, was being investigated in 1521 or so, and he began to mutter things like "we're all equal with God" and was immediately investigated by the reformation –the Spanish Inquisition, from which he escapes. Six months later he's captured by the Calvinists who are the Protestant movement, against the Pope, who after a trial, literally burn him. So he was burned by both the Calvin-Protestants and by the Pope. That would be the condition in which you find yourself. The mind that denies—never mind the manner of denial. You're teaching any denial is an attack on God.

Thanks for letting me teach the Bible class. When you're trying to teach this in space/time, you teach you're playing the character of Jesus. You actually walk on to a scenario of objective associations and declare yourself to be the Christ. That will work perfectly since you are the Christ. Obviously it's a new script in the association. Just as obviously, you will be written out of that script. What you will do inevitably is start your own company of actors –which is nothing but a different time –I'm trying to convert the effects of that rather than converting my own mind. But very initially you may attempt to convert the effects of your own mind because they appear to be the cause of your problem. That is the nature of man in relationship with himself. All I can tell you is: It's All An Illusion. As long as you remain trapped in a spatial/temporal separation, you cannot know the totality of space/time, which is what you are really undergoing. And that would be all that you have to do.

The nice thing about this association, now that we're communicating in mind, when the resurrection occurs, the circle includes the association. We don't give a crap what your physical body is. We don't even care if you're determined to be sick. Guys, I'm teaching you energy reassociation. All you would have to do is put up with me for another minute and you'll be in Heaven. The manner in which you deny does not concern us in the slightest. What in hell do we care the manner in which you have denied you are perfect as God created you. It's your determination to establish the manner of your denial and acceptance that bind you here. It's the whole *Course In Miracles*. You cannot not be perfect.

When this intensity of the necessity to teach, or the acknowledgment of the transformation grows in you, it will always be an expression of a phenomenon that supersedes or comes before your old association. It will always be greater and greater as you progress in this because you are a comparison. And for a lot of you this may very well become very intense. You're determined to teach: "Hey, I'm having an experience of God! The value system that I used to have is no longer of value to me." At that point, obviously, you are the greatest threat to the value system of your previous projections. All I can tell you is that it is all in your mind. All I'm really telling you is that there is nothing outside of you. Ideas leave not their source and whatever you are trapped in will be a product or an acknowledgment or transformation or projection or an extension of your own association with yourself. Say WOW! What a threatening message!

You want to know what the threatening message is? **YOU ARE NOT GUILTY!** The most devastating message you could ever get. You are actually attempting to teach that you are not guilty. I know this is the whole *Course In Miracles.* Literally you cannot be guilty of being separate from God. If that is so, anything you do would be in your own mind, no matter how you term it in judgment—good, bad, evil, wonderful, will have nothing at all to do with your creative mind. You cannot be guilty of separation. That is the message that the world is most fearful to hear.

What happens when you leave Light in an association is it has nothing to do with conceptions at all. Everyone who comes into the Light, it makes no difference where he came from or what he thought he is, will begin to have the experience. In that sense you have left a location. But in a deep sense, it is nothing but a transient holy instant. It's a holy instant that remains available in all circumstances. But when an aggregation occurs, it creates a spatial association that emanates out in energy of love and forgiveness. Suddenly, someone can be doing virtually anything, and he'll go, "oh, the hell with this." It happens for no reason whatsoever. It's an example of a miracle. It doesn't happen because of anything he does. You, as atonement teachers of God, have presented to the association the bright identities of our mutual love for God and each other. That's called forgiveness. And that's how this works. Why anyone as a Christian would stand up and teach the Old Testament is entirely beyond me. You have heard it said an eye for an eye, I say yes, but that is not what this is. This is the declaration that God is Love and that your need to get even with your brother is an attack on God. Don't do that. You can't get even with perfection. Don't carry that resentment with you. If you do, you're going to be condemned to the effects of your own mind. You're inflicting pain on yourself in order to verify your existent association. How absurd. All of the deniers of this simple message have fundamental problems with the admission that they are the cause of their own pain. That is they have no objection to being the cause somewhere of their own pleasure, but they object to being the cause of their own pain. The key to salvation is that you are doing this to yourself. That made me very happy. I don't know if that relieved me entirely of the resentment for my brother, but certainly it made me accept the idea that whatever he was doing I didn't have to react to it if I didn't want to. That was the beginning of how this works. In my own mind I am perfect as God created me. Why would I let some other human being out there tell me what I am? I'll accept responsibility. I may experience pain and call it sacrifice in the process, but at least I've located the cause of the problem. The solution then must be in there somewhere. I can continue to crucify myself if I choose to. But I'm contained within my own mind in that moment of fear. I love you guys. See you tomorrow.

Some of you guys bring your old grievances. You come into the provision of this spatial reference and you begin to very rapidly undergo experiences of your own transformation. Or, if you bring your own transformation into spatial references of attack, they may well begin to experience you. The idea that you could have a location of salvation, a location of Light is actually what the second coming is. Because until then you had to be a transient teacher with staff and sandals going out into the world. That's the whole teaching of Jesus. Because any establishment in the temporal frame you're in would be corrupt by its very nature. Now you are teaching pure temple of God. You are saying you can take a temple of corruption, that is limited attack, definitions, cause and effect, and convert that —square the circle, four square and divide it into Holy Spirit perpendicularly and that you would have a Masonic Temple.

And I will give unto thee
the keys of the kingdom of heaven:
and whatsoever thou shalt bind on earth
shall be bound in heaven:
and whatsoever thou shalt loose on earth
shall be loosed in heaven.

CHAPTER SIX

The Keys To The Kingdom

The need of the animal man to have a God is evident in everything he does. The solution to the problem of the search for that perfect, universal mind will always be contained somewhere within the aggregation of the association. The question is never whether man is seeking a solution to the problem –three things would be involved:

1. The admission of the totality of the Universal Mind.

2. The position or the relationship of the individual man with God.

3. If man is separate from God, the manner in which he can come to be with God.

This is catechism. I always remember when the Catholic kids got to go to catechism, and as a Protestant kid, I would have liked to go to catechism: I'm going to learn about God. Well, this is learning about God. We are going to learn, in a very fundamental association of us, if it really is possible, through the auspices of Jesus Christ of Nazareth, a risen man, who came to know God according to the legends and the traditions of the Jewish religion, that there is a God, a man—born man—who did three things:

1. He admitted to the totality of the power of God.

2. He then came to know the power of his mind to recognize that in association with himself.

3. And he proclaimed to you the necessity for the transformation of your mind in order to do it.

This is all that Jesus of Nazareth has ever said, and is very obviously all that the human condition of society has rejected in #1, #2 or #3 aspects of this necessity. What is #1: There is a God. Is that God totally loving, perfect and eternally creative? Generally, you can get some sort of unanimity in the statement: Yes, there is a divine, whole, creating God. Say yes! Look at it with me. If you go into a catechism and begin to teach to the Christian in the church, there cannot be more than these three things that you will address to him, very simply because that's the only three things there are. There cannot be more than God and you and the manner of coming to God.

Come on, get in the spirit. Getting into spirit would be either #2 or #3. In the spirit I will begin to communicate with you the power of my mind to relate with God. Never will there be more or less than those. If I simplify that, it would be the Father, the Son and the Holy Spirit —the power of God, the son struggling and the spirit. Now if you want to read this with me, students of the Bible, in effect you could go into any Christian church and pick up the New Testament —I promise you could do this —and teach it. You think somehow that there is something esoteric about the teachings of Jesus in regard to this. There's nothing esoteric about it at all. All He will say are these three things. Obviously there's a little embroidering in the translation, so if you go into a catechism or class and they demand that you interpret that for them, you interpret it by saying He means what He says. That will still be a form of interpretation to the perceptual mind, but at least you are setting the terms under which, if you are in this catechism of coming to know God through what you would call the auspices of a risen man identified as Jesus, you will discover that all He ever said —ALL, all He ever says —is that there is a perfect loving God; that the power of your mind is the power of God projected; and that there is a manner in which you can come to know that is true, which is rejected in a fundamental sense. The manner of coming to know God is rejected in the fundamental sense because the essence of man is the rejection of the fundamental coming to know God.

It's an amazing idea. If I stand up here now, and speak to you in a little more modern vernacular, and express Jesus of Nazareth, you see where you as a Christian reject it. I'm curious. God makes all things perfect and you cannot not be a part of that. If you appear to be separate from God, you must be using the power of God's mind to retain your separation. If you are using the power of God's mind to retain your separation, through the reassociation of your own mind, you may direct that power to the certainty that you are perfect as God created you. And since you are trapped in some sort of containment of self, there must be a manner of transformation where you can come to do it. If you'll let all of the associations in the New Testament be directed to this, it will become very obvious that this is what Jesus is teaching.

You're looking for something complicated. It's not. You'll find that scripture says this. Here's the difficulty in it: When Jesus stands up –when you stand up to teach this –you're not going to have any problem perhaps in the admission that there is an almighty God creating eternally. And you may not even have a problem in their admission that this is not it. The problem that must arise is the responsibility of the individual human's association in regard to the power of the universe and his basic rejection of the power of his own mind. There is never an indication of Jesus in the New Testament –never, it's not there –that you are not responsible for this. It's not there. Yet nothing is more insidiously rejected by the Christian establishment than the totality of the responsibility of the individual mind for what is going on outside of it. This is the entire *Course In Miracles*, and if you care to look at it the entire teachings of Jesus Christ. There is no way where He does not teach not only that the power of your mind is binding you to earthly conditions, but that quite literally, if you're willing to accept it, the power of your mind binds Heaven to you. That must be rejected.

I picked up *Jesus is Praying* that we're putting out. Have you seen *Jesus is Speaking?* We're beginning to publish. This is *Jesus is Praying.* If I opened up *Jesus is Praying*, and I'm going to direct your attention to your capacity of the third association, that it is possible for you, through the transformation of your mind, to have a contact with God. I would have to indicate somewhere in this booklet that you are responsible for the actions of your own mind, and that through the transformation of that mind, you can come to know that *you* are the Kingdom of Heaven. It doesn't seem, when you pick up the New Testament, that this is what it says. But this is only true because the human condition is a concerted effort not to use the power of its own mind. I don't care whether they do or not, but please don't tell me that the risen Christ did not teach it. What I don't want to be told is that Jesus did not say this. What I also do not want to be told is that Jesus did not mean this. I have a right, in my own mind as a Christian to say I believe He meant that. I believe He meant this: "I will give unto you the keys of the Kingdom of Heaven." Jesus said that."I will give them to you." He said it again and again."I share with you the admission that we are perfect as God created us." Then later on He's going to say that you will go on and give to your brother. That's Christianity. But first: "Accept what I am giving you." Look out!"The keys to the Kingdom of Heaven." Listen to what He says now: "And whatsoever thou shalt bind on earth shall be bound in Heaven." (Mat. 16:19)

Now I don't know where the Christian theologians handle this, but anyone who would look at it would have to say that you are being given, personally, the power to use your mind to retain the retention of yourself in your own limitation and by that factoring literally deny yourself Heaven.

When you go out to teach this catechism and you read that, I want you to stop and I want you to say to that pupil: what does He mean by that? At that point, Christianity, hopefully, through *A Course In Miracles*, may become suddenly very exciting to the Christian. Instead of just being a Sunday morning escape where he comes socially, he will say: do you mean that there is an activity going on through the recognition of the resurrection, whereby I can make application of the power of my mind to come to know that there is a God? That's all really Jesus asks you to do, isn't it? What an idea that a man 2000 years ago stood up and said that! What a second idea that it has survived translations for 2000 years. And what an amazing third idea that it's totally rejected by everyone in this association of temporal mind.

... Not only shall be bound in Heaven, but KEY, whatsoever thou shalt loose —release from the bondage of your mind —on earth shall be loosed in Heaven. Is that too complicated for you? Is that too fearful for you? Well, it's fearful because you suddenly have been given the power of your own mind. I only gave you the power of your own mind through the power of God. I didn't take away from you the power of your own mind to be evil and be self contained. Instead I gave you the power through God to do exactly what you decide to do, with the admonition that you're going to be responsible for it. Now, somewhere along the line you don't mind the power of your own mind, but you don't like the idea that you're going to be responsible for it. That's the fact of the matter. It's incredible.

Now, I'm going to give you the power of your own mind: God is the Mind with which I think. I may make application of that power in any way that I choose, but I sure as hell, in hell, am going to get the result of that in my own mind. As I sow I'm going to reap. This is the whole teaching of Jesus. He says nothing but this. There's nothing really mystical about this. He says wherever you make the application of the power of your own mind, you're going to get the result of it. If you limit the association with yourself, you'll get that result. If you let go and allow the power of God to come about, you will see that you are perfect as God created you.

As to the third association, the manner in which you do it: very simply, you must be born again. There is no manner in which you can come to know this without being born in the spirit. There is no manner in which you can come to know this, without perhaps directing your attention to the necessity for the resurrection of the body, where it will say that your whole body must be Light. And you're going to teach in catechism that this means that you must undergo the transformation of your body. And they'll say that they are very fearful of doing that. You must be born again. It's going to teach you that Jesus is always with you because He is a brother of Love and has been with you forever. How simple is this solution. The method of communication is for you to take the admission of the power of God to use the power of your mind in association with what appears to be outside of you in a continuing contact through the transformation of your mind with God.

Question: Why hasn't this been taught heretofore in your association? It's pretty obvious that what I'm teaching you is so. At least it's so from the standpoint of the teachings of Jesus. Certainly it's true from a philosophical, reasonable standpoint. Your mind says:

1. There is a God, and you are separate.

2. But you can't divide the power, so the power of your mind to make that decision must be yours.

3. So there must be a method that you come to it that transcends your association with yourself.

Well, how come no one on this earth that I can find actually is practicing or coming to know this? Why? Why hasn't the world come to know this? Because until you do, it can't. You guys want to complicate things. You find yourself in a place where the world has obviously rejected this fundamental teaching. And you keep saying: what's the matter with the world? Why can't the world come to know this? You don't like the solution to that. Because the solution is the problem of this world. And it's not different in you than it is in anyone else. Obviously, until you change your mind, until you step forward as a follower of Jesus, you cannot know that as Jesus directs you, you are the savior of the world. If this sentence does not say that you personally are the savior of the world, what in hell does it say? What does it say except the power of the saviorship of the world not only is you, but depends on you in your chaotic association to come about. So now the solution has become simple because the application of the third: "Know ye not that ye must be born again?" allows you to direct your attention to the very simple necessity of the personal transformation of you in your relationship with Jesus. Is that so? Yes.

Not a priesthood, guys. Not going out and teaching that we must all come to know, I'm sorry that's not what it is. If you're going to be a Christian, you're going to teach personal transformation. I love priests. I've always had a fundamental love for priests because somewhere in them they are searching as you have searched for the truth. And they even have attempted to isolate themselves from the world in order to find within their association an answer. Obviously, they must accept first the fundamental admission (#2) that the power is within them. Now, they admit that the power is within them, and identify themselves as being capable of associating with evil in regard to the power of their own mind. They then find themselves sinful. As though somehow the human condition could actually be verified in a universal mind as having the capacity to commit evil. This is where the separation occurs.

That is not to say that those associations cannot accept, in their own personal pursuit of God, the admission of the necessity for their contact through prayer of their own minds with the mind of God. That's our teaching. And that's how you present it to them.

We seem to find that the religious associations are so embedded in the priesthood that you may feel that there is no hope for them. We may discover very soon that is not true. These are seekers unto God. I saw an article that "Bullock's Retreat Sparks Concern." All the priests are coming up to Chula Vista Resort from the diocese and somebody is complaining that they should stay down there and do it because it costs so much. This whole article is how much money it costs for the priests coming to Chula Vista. It would be nice to invite them to The Cheese Factory for some Brother Lawrence Strudel. We've got a new cookbook, and one of the recipes will be from the Franciscan, Brother Lawrence, who was the divine cook. Or give them a cup of cappuccino. All of them will be one aspect of their determination to recognize God: if they're Jesuits, they will demand that you forego sin and listen to Jesus; if they're Franciscans, they'll teach only love God and never mind. We're all a part of those associations.

What are you really teaching: The method of the conversion of my mind through my constant determination to figure out what in hell is going on here. This is the whole *Course in Miracles*. Rather than staying in this chaotic association, I will direct my attention, continually, to the transformation of my own mind.

At the beginning of this little booklet, *Jesus is Praying*, I was writing this morning. It will say very simply that this is a vehicle of communication and admission of God: I can't and He will. It is simple logic. This is what Jesus says here: God cannot give you more than you ask for. The little intro will say that God can't give you more than you ask for, and you ask for far too little. But if you ask for everything you've got to be willing to accept it. There's a certain danger in teaching the power of your mind, but not if you admit that the power comes from God. If that's true, you would make no assertions at all in regard to yourself because you would not want the responsibility of the power of your own mind in what is going to occur. But by denying the power of your own mind, you can make assertions that verify you in temporal identity, and reject others and place them onto the responsibility of your brother. Nonsense. The emphasis of the teaching today is only on your personal transformation. The emphasis of Jesus in *A Course in Miracles* and the New Testament is only on the necessity of your admission that there is a God, that you can use the power of your own mind to know that's true, and to apply the application of that transformation to come to it.

That's pretty exciting. If you'll bear those things in mind, and make application of them to yourself, they will be readily available to you when you are confronted by an association, if you intend to teach. #1 will be easy. #2 will be difficult in regard to the admission that it is possible for the association to actually sin within it's own association without God knowing about it. Certainly #3 is the transformation of your mind.

"Lo, I am always with you." Is that true? YES! It is true that God is an experience. Don't I have to identify it as experience? In all of this teaching, everyone has sinned and fallen short. In all of this teaching there is a fundamental necessity to decide that you want this. You cannot know the power of your own mind very simply because it is beyond belief. But that is not to say that since you are a believer in something that you cannot take that belief and direct it to your determination to enter Heaven and be perfect as God created you. I mean that literally. I mean that somewhere you fake it until you make it. I mean that somewhere, since you don't know the power of your own mind, to be in this classroom, you must have made a decision that there is an alternative. While you may not have known what it is, you are being persistent in your determination to have this experience. I am here to assure you through my mind, or through Jesus' mind, or through your mind, or through your brother's mind, that nothing in the universe can stop you from doing this if you accept the fundamental admission that the power of your own mind is what is setting the terms for the condition of the universe. Now this is all that Jesus said 2000 years ago, and it's all that I'm telling you now. It's only your rejection of it that's holding you in hell.

This is the transformation part: "Behold, I show you a mystery: we will all suddenly be changed." And all transformed minds know that they were suddenly changed. Suddenly the power of their mind entered into the association with God and they experienced it.

I need to ask you a question. I don't have any answer to this. Everybody is always talking about "voices." A voice speaks to me. Yet, I'm told that hearing voices is not considered by the human condition to be a very desirable thing. What's the matter with you? You're hearing voices? But that's the whole teaching. Everybody hears voices. Jesus hears voices. The disciples hear voices. Paul hears voices. The Course says listen to this voice, you'll be told by this voice exactly what to do. I didn't hear any voices... well, I might have heard some. Hearing somebody else's voice doesn't do you a lot of good. Even if you do hear it, you don't necessarily know how it applies to you. You're walking in the super market and you're hearing voices. And everybody says: what's the matter. And you say: I'm hearing voices. Be careful with that. You're liable to hear things like "your kingdom is not of this world." You're liable to hear things like "you're perfect as God created you." You're liable to hear things like "what are you doing in hell?" You're liable to hear things like "it's me, Jesus, standing beside you."

I find that the application of letting Jesus or the Holy Spirit decide never worked for me. Eeny, meany, miney, moe never worked. The admonition "let the voice speak to you" or "let the Holy Spirit decide" really didn't work. And the reason it doesn't work is because I have retained the limitation within my own mind as to what I expect the Holy Spirit to decide for me. If I'm in the frozen food section trying to decide whether to have cauliflower or peas, and I stand there and say "I'll let the Holy Spirit decide." That is not to say that the Holy Spirit is not deciding... the decision that is being made in my mind to verify, whether I eat cauliflower or peas, the purpose for which I am eating the peas, will determine the efficacy of the choice that I make. Once I have decided I want to do that, any application could be made.

I was just looking at the inevitability of the mystical experience, just for a second, and how nervous and fearful the associations become when you begin to realign your mind with the universal mind, and how the aspects of that realignment will be termed a form of unbalance or literally the loss of your balance in association with yourself. Of course, that's true. And of course, we are preparing now to deal with it in the new continuum of time. We will be dealing with very rapid destabilization of the human condition. We're going to have holding tanks. Some of you still need a holding tank. At the Healing Center it's very likely that you're going to get associations who are not going to wait to submit all of their application to come to the Academy. Suddenly a voice speaks to them and says: "I am the Lord," and you'll have a tendency to say: "I'm sure they're all right." That will always be associated with the guilt of the message you're teaching yourself. Be of good cheer, there is a God.

That's our catechism:

1. The wholeness of God creating.

2. The power of your mind. All power is given unto you under Heaven and earth, there's nothing you cannot do, including the responsibility for it.

3. The necessity for the transformation.

How does that form in your mind? Many of you now are beginning to undergo the experience through the catechism of the communication through prayer and voice –the other pamphlet, *Jesus is Speaking, Listen.* Remember that you have invented language to retain the identity of yourself in correspondence with yourself. Can we use *Jesus is Speaking*, can we use that language? Of course. Why? The power of God is the power of your mind. The admission of that power is what salvation is. If it got any simpler, we wouldn't be here at all. How do you feel with an advanced student who suddenly disappears? If there's no smell of sulfur, you're probably all right.

Imagine 150 lovely priests who have dedicated their lives to the necessity of the retention of sin and the remission of it. And you can give them the attention of love by offering them a piece of Brother Lawrence Strudel. In the teachings of Jesus there is nothing that will not give them total entrance to Heaven –by the consumption of the strudel? This is the whole teaching of Jesus. Everything is divine. Won't that reduce to some sort of strudel-eating ceremony? It cannot not. You disappear into Light and to the remaining associations you have become Strudel Eaters –the application of the method by which you do it is all the recognition you'll be given. Once that has been determined in the mind, the establishment can determine whether they want to associate with you or not.

The sad thing about the Adventists this year is that they have been reduced in their numbers. We would prefer that there would be a million of them. But the necessity of the admission of the New Covenant will reduce the numbers. It isn't that the fire and brimstone is not necessary –I love it. I love the idea that this is hell. And it is more possible for these associations, in the Advent-isms, to admit to than the necessity for the New Covenant –"Jesus is love: give everything away and come home with me." The manner in which you escape hell *is* the New Covenant. So the number of Adventists has been very strongly reduced. But that's okay. You are introducing them to the teachings of Jesus, of the certainty of your transformation. Of course it's fire and hell and brimstone. That's what this is.

Of course you have to hate this place, there is no other way out. Of course you have to make a decision for God that includes the rejection of this world. I'm sorry, guys, but that's the teaching of the necessity for the power of your own mind to redirect itself to Heaven rather than to this. Is that part of the Jesus teaching rejected? Totally and absolutely. If it were not rejected, there would be no such place as this. The decision to stay in this place is being made by you in the correspondence of your own mind. Taken out of context, the idea that you have to hate your mother and your father and your brother doesn't make much sense. But if you'll be inclusive with it (you've got to hate the world), that makes perfect sense. "Yeah, but I've got to hate myself then, too." Yes, you may hate yourself if you wish. But remember, I am giving you the power to change your mind. You may then retain the power to hate yourself and God or change your mind and love Him. The power remains yours. What isn't love is fear. I'm teaching the Course to show you not only how uncompromisingly you must teach it, but how uncompromisingly it was taught by Jesus of Nazareth and how certain you can become that no compromise is possible if:

1. You are perfect as God created you,

2. You have the power to change your mind and

3. You admit the necessity for the transformation.

See how valid these things are. They will hold perfectly. There is nothing you can say about the condition of the existence of temporal associations compared to eternity that will not be these three things.

That's regardless of the religion, regardless of the philosophy. What have we got? We've got singularity, we've got separation, and we've got a manner of coming to know there's a God. That's it. That's what this little book will say. This will include the admission —it's through Jesus:

1. The admission that there is a loving God, eternally creating,

2. That you have the power within you, all power is given unto you in Heaven and in earth, you may take the teachings of this man and do greater things with them in the power of your own mind as you remain here for a moment, and

3. You're going to continue to have the experience of the transformation of your body/mind.

This will say I don't know how to handle the idea that your body must become Light. Jesus says that His message is Light. He's talking about Light. About the transformation of the cells of your body. Can you teach that? Know ye not ye must be born again?

This should start being kind of fun for you. There's no way you can fail at it. God creates forever. You are a total part of that. I didn't subtract you from sin. I'm not concerned about your sin in the slightest. I'm saying you may use the power of your own mind to separate yourself from God. This is chapter 3 of *A Course In Miracles* I'd like to have you review that. There's a description of the ego in chapter 3 that shouldn't be overlooked. Obviously you have the power of your mind to decide you want to do this. What a lovely idea that you can have the experience and change your mind and be with God.

There are some things that are necessary and are being augmented now. I'm trying to keep this down just for a second. I don't see any reason you couldn't do this. Any difficulty that you have with this, advanced teachers, will be a continuing application of the retention of yourself using the power of your mind. The reason that's tricky is because it's tricky. It's a tricky association because in the first two things I've given you the power of God and also the power of your own mind. That's always the point where the maximum conflict occurs. Do you hear me? You can always judge an unhealed teacher by his determination to foster on you the recognition of what he sees himself as in the definition of his own transformation. That's a little tricky. A completely open mind has come to know, this is Jesus teaching, that his kingdom is not of this world. I direct you to my mind. I have no correspondence with the world at all. That is to say, the manner in which I am attempting to teach you is not an establishment of my mind determined on what I am in relationship to God.

I would never fire and brimstone you without giving you the salvation of your own mind. The necessity for the confrontation is evident in all of the teachings – the tipping over of the tables, the setting free of the doves – you need that confrontation. But not that the solution is in the establishment of the savior. The savior is not an establishment, he's (#3) a continuing transformation, or admission of that power, that then flows through him without his retention of it. Most certainly if an unhealed teacher retains the definition of his association, he will foster in his own projections a demonstration of his capacity of confrontation with who? Himself! Aaah. If you emulate the teachings of an awakened man and do confrontations, you better be ready to release them in love. Step back, or surer than heck you're going to establish a relationship which demands love in conflict. Remember this, the conflict could only be in your own mind. Don't emulate anyone. Just open your hearts. You are at a final step here because this is the only step you really take. Why would you want to have anything to do with your own teachings anyway? Your own teachings have nothing at all to do with it, they're only an expedience that is necessary because the association believes that choice is possible. Obviously something is fundamentally wrong with the idea that you could take the power of God's mind and limit yourself in your own mind. That has to be fundamentally impossible. And just as obviously, you believe that the choice is possible. So you are given the power of your mind to make that choice.

This has been a fun week. A lot of lovely stuff is going on in Holland. Lots of experiences of our own transformation. Just as certainly there's nothing I can do, nothing you can do, nothing anyone can do, if you are determined to remain in a mind set where you are fundamentally unwilling to admit the momensity of what is going on in your current situation. I don't know where the answer to that is.

I know that I am amazed constantly by the mind sets of the human condition. I don't know –in the Course Jesus says we just smile and say we don't know. There's a lovely consciousness that you may have known historically. A couple of weeks ago we got back five *Jesus is Speaking* from her. The little note says: thank you very much for these, but you sent me too many. It was done kindly. It said: I am returning these so someone else can have them... or whatever the reason. But it certainly wasn't done with any malice. She appreciated the 10 copies that she had, but that was sufficient. It's hard for me to understand that in her mind that is a booklet. There is no notation in her mind that that is Jesus speaking! It's a booklet *about* Jesus speaking. They're free. If she got the booklet *Jesus is Speaking* and says Jesus is speaking! and she would go out and at the minimum give the books away. But she sent them back. To that association that's a perfectly natural thing to do. WOW! Jesus is objective. There is no admission in her that that book is not some sort of a symbol of what Jesus would say to her.

We have tape listeners. When they get a tape that is too noisy, they send it back and say: send me a tape that is not quite so noisy. I love your tapes... and they list 8 or 9 tapes... and they send back the noisy one back with a note that says: evidently you are instructing them to be noisy. They don't make application of the reference of Jesus, or what the teaching is, to themselves. They hold it objective, and establish a relationship between themselves. That's the human condition. To you the idea of the objectivity of the message finally is becoming silly since the whole teaching is only your own personal transformation, not an association of it.

Leave here with the certainty that nothing will be outside of you. You are perfect as God created you. The power of mind is yours. I am responsible for this. I get what I ask for. That's the prayer book: any time that I would become totally dependent on God, I will be in Heaven. Very simple. And crucially, the necessity for your experience with God.

What the hell good is God going to do you if you refuse to experience Him. God is the experience of Love. You say to me: I am not experiencing Him. I hate to tell you, but the reason for not experiencing Him is that you would rather experience yourself. This is where the obstacle lies. This is chapter 3 –the idea that the association is using the power of his own mind to deny his own perfection and be somehow in competition or in continuing experience of an authority problem –which is what the separation would have to be. If you will accept you're using the power of the mind, you must have a very fundamental authority problem in regard to who's in charge of the universe. You are somewhere refusing to take entire charge of the universe. If you did you would be successful in being entirely evil. You've been working on it for a very long time. It won't work. You can't be entirely evil. The definition of evil is partiality. If you could be entirely evil, you'd be perfect. You'd have nothing to compare your evilness with. That's the teaching of the totality of spatial relationships –true perception. It says very simply that if you don't exclude anything from yourself you'll experience a glorious moment of total evil, or the schism. At that time, you'll be totally perfect. You may live in that totality at this moment in time.

I've offered you the freedom of "not guilty." The whole basis of *A Course In Miracles* is no matter what you do you are not going to be guilty for it. But if you do anything you will be responsible for it in its entirety. There's no question that God is guilty of creating the universe and you perfectly. But why would you have to call it guilt? Certainly God has created a son who can become totally guilty with Him. You are guilty of being perfectly you.

I am the resurrection, and the life:
he that believeth in me,
though he were dead, yet shall he live:
And whosoever liveth and believeth in me
shall never die. Believest thou this?

CHAPTER SEVEN

Know Ye Not
Ye Must Be Born Again?

What continually surprises me is the ability of the human being to ignore or misdirect or deny the direct teachings that are coming from *A Course In Miracles.* It is simply and wholly the entire teaching and demonstration of Jesus Christ of Nazareth –the capacity to heal through conceptual transformation of His mind, and the demonstration of His physical resurrection.

If Christianity is not the physical resurrection of you as an associate of the totality of the acknowledgment of the resurrection of Jesus Christ, what is it? We're teaching your personal resurrection.

We're going to consider some of the historic personages or disciples of Jesus, namely Peter and John. First, a look at Judaism. The *temple* was both the political and the religious authority of the world, which it was. The variation of that is inevitable, since the assertion of the temple as a political necessity, what you would call an ethical or moral or cultural necessity; the deviation from the temple is, and was, inevitable, since the assertion of the temple as a political necessity has a tendency to subtract itself entirely from God or the necessity for personal contact and transformation. Actually a movement, in what you would call Sanhedrin, or Sadducees –I'm doing Judaism here for a minute, from the certainty of Moses of his direct contact with God

—has a natural tendency for man to define within his own relationships culturally what God must be so he can verify the establishment. Inevitably, there will occur within any temple association what you would call a Pharisaical rebellion. You don't have to be a Biblical scholar to understand this.

Let's take the Pharisee. Pharisee means deviant, or as it became, "separatist." In about 156 BC, in the beginning of the Second Commonwealth, the Pharisee, which literally means *deviant,* said: No! Moses teaches that we can contact God directly, and that we can undergo an experience of resurrection and that we can be born again. That's the whole teaching of the Pharisee. There's no question that the Pharisee teaches what amounts to reincarnation, what results in the determination that man can actually contact God directly. That's what a Pharisee is. He is a deviant from the temple. In modern Judaism, at its fundamental commercial level, is a Pharisaical denial of the temple —that is, the formulation of what we term church or synagogue. Synagogue is separate from the temple or the laws, in that it indicates the capacity for man to engage in dialogue concerning his association with God. Quite literally, spiritual intellectual discussions are allowed and encouraged in Pharisaical identities, so that you and I can confront each other about what God is, including the admission of the possibility for our transformation. Jesus, growing up as a Jew, was very much aware of the teaching of the Pharisee. Today you might call Him a Protest-ant, somebody who said: No! I can undergo this experience directly as taught in the scriptures.

The problem was not that so much, the problem was because the Pharisee was teaching scripture, he was determined that contained within the scripture would be a method by which he could come to do that. And along comes Jesus of Nazareth. He said: no, there is no way within the scripture, except as the scripture teaches through the necessity for the transformation of mind, that there is any manner by which you can do this. St. Paul, who dramatically experienced the transformation of his self identity, says: good works will avail you nothing. While the Pharisee wants to have an association separate from the establishment, somewhere within the congeniality of his identity he insists that works will avail him in the process to return to God. You might be surprised to see how what we call history continually repeats itself in the necessity for the human being, first to become a Pharisee, and then to deny the necessity for his own personal transformation. .

Very obviously, the Pharisee teaches the resurrection of Jesus Christ. He says: let's examine the process by which Jesus comes to do this. Let's study it. He is a deviant from the temple in that he says resurrection is a possibility contained within the individual, with the pretended ignorance of the necessity for *his* individual transformation –which is all that Jesus teaches.

Jesus doesn't fool around in the Course when He says: God is my Father, and He loves His Son. I want you to know that all Jesus ever said was: **therefore, be ye perfect, even as your Father in Heaven is perfect.** (Matthew 5:48) Most particularly, He did not say: study the method by which I do this, which the Pharisee is obviously determined to do.

An example of the Pharisaical association is Peter. Peter says: Jesus, I know you, I'm going to follow you to the end of time. Jesus says: no, you're going to deny me. Peter says: no, I'm never going to. Jesus says: yes you are. How was Jesus so certain? Because Peter was sure he wasn't going to. Jesus was very much aware that He had been set up as an idol. John, the mystical association, is very much aware that Peter does this. I'll read this to you out of John. When Jesus says: someone is going to deny me. Peter says: I'll never do that. John says: Will it be me, Lord? Can you hear this? This is a direct quote from the gospel of John. I'll read that to you because it is very interesting. Jesus, at the end of His worldly sojourn, as recorded by John, says to Peter: "feed my sheep." Peter says: "I'm going to." He says to him again: "Peter, teach what I tell you." Peter says: "I'm going to." He says it to him a third time. Finally, Peter gets a little irritated. He declares to Jesus: "I'm telling you I'm going to teach all about you." Then He says: "You are going to grow old teaching this and you are going to retain the establishment as evidence of your determination."

In the last part of John, when John admits who he is –the Love of Jesus, as Jesus' singular brother, John says: I was the guy who said: will it be me? This is the admission that he is imperfect in his time association. Jesus handles that by saying: teach this, teach forgiveness in the discipline so that you can come to know that you are me. Certainly, that step would have to be made if you were to read Lesson 224: *My true Identity is so secure, so lofty, sinless, glorious and great, wholly beneficent and free from guilt, that Heaven looks to It to give it light.* You are the light of the world! How is Heaven different than earth? Jesus says it's not if it is light. Heaven looks to it to give it light. *It lights the world as well. It is the gift my Father gave to me; the one as well I give the world. There is no gift but This that can be either given or received.* There is no gift but the light of the world, and the certainty of your perfection, as created by God, that can be given or received. **This is reality, and only This.** Therefore, be perfect as your Father in Heaven is perfect. Your kingdom is not of this world. You must undergo the experience of the resurrection of your association of temporalness or objective reality. *This is illusion's end. It is the truth. My name, O Father, still is known to You. I have forgotten it, and do not know where I am going, who I am, or what it is I do. Remind me, Father, now, for I am weary of the world I see. Reveal what You would have me see instead.*

The Pharisee says: isn't that interesting. We've got a guy in our temple teaching that man is undergoing a great experience; that man, the species, is going to come to know this. The Pharisee says: how wonderful that in the scripture it says that man will perfect himself, that he will undergo continuing lives – that's what the Pharisee taught – so that he can come to know God.

Now let's go to the gospel of John and see how John would address the idea of a Pharisee, who is in a fundamental denial of the necessity for individual and personal transformation of the body. Is that what Jesus teaches? Here you are facing anyone teaching conceptually. You are teaching physical resurrection through your experience of it, and you've got a guy who says: boy that's really important to me. Certainly all of the scriptures say that man must undergo that experience and I can certainly see that you are teaching that experience. The Pharisees will say that to you. He is liable not to say it in the temple. He is liable, maybe, to call you on the phone and say: I see you are teaching directly what *A Course In Miracles* says, and people are really having experiences of contact with God. How do you do that? Let's read it:

There was a man of the Pharisees, named Nicodemus, a ruler of the Jews. (John 3:1) He was at a high level of association in the synagogue. The same came to Jesus by night –obviously, because he was very much aware that not only was Jesus teaching separatism, but somewhere He was willing to declare it in his own association. Although the Pharisee did not want to go that far, he wanted somehow to declare his admiration for the audacity of a man who was willing to stand up and teach that: your kingdom is not of this world. Why? Because the Pharisee wanted to know how He came to know that. Very obviously, anyone teaching *A Course In Miracles* will look at you and say: how did you come to know that? Because I read *A Course In Miracles,* and it promised me the experience and I had it! How did you come to know this? It says it. Oh. You see the same thing going on here. Nicodemus says: Rabbi, great teacher, we (singularity absolutely escapes him) know that thou art come from God –at least under the terms we are willing to admit. Now tell us under what terms God spoke to you. How did you use the scriptures to discover God?

God has obviously spoken directly to you.... for no man can do these miracles that thou doest, except God be with him. (John 3:2) He's saying: boy, you're doing a lot of stuff. Where did you find in the scripture how to do this? We're teaching what you're teaching. How did you come to know this? How are you able to work miracles?

Jesus answered and said unto him: Verily, verily, I say unto thee, Except a man be born again, he cannot see the kingdom of God. (John 3:3) He doesn't answer him at all. He has nothing to say to him about how God directed Him to do it. He says you've got to undergo the experience of being born again. Isn't that true? He doesn't say God gave me power to do this. He says that through the experience of my own transformation I am transforming the world.

What I want to be sure of is that you understand that unhealed teachers are not teaching *A Course In Miracles*. I want you to see that.

Nicodemus saith unto him, How can a man be born when he is old? Can he enter the second time into his mother's womb, and be born? Listen. The answer is very peculiar. It's a particular kind of answer: Jesus answered, Verily, verily, I say unto thee, Except a man be born of water *and* of the Spirit, he cannot enter into the kingdom of God. (John 3:5) This is the direct admission for the Pharisee to understand: I must practice the discipline through the baptism of the water and the admission of the necessity for the transformation in order to have the experience. That is, I cannot be born of the spirit unless I am born of the water. I'm sorry, that's just the fact of the matter. This is the whole teaching of *A Course In Miracles*. You must take the application of the power of your mind to be baptized in the water in order to see that the spirit and the water are the same singular idea. In other words, the Pharisee is perfectly willing to admit to the possibility within the relationship, but not to the necessity for him to direct his attention to the rebirth, and to have the experience. Therefore, he cannot enter into the kingdom of God.

That which is born of the flesh is flesh; and that which is born of the Spirit is spirit. Marvel not that I said unto thee, Ye must be born again. The wind bloweth where it listeth, and thou hearest the sound thereof, but canst not tell whence it cometh, and whither it goeth; so is everyone that is born of the Spirit. (John 3:6-8) What He says is: you don't know nothing! Stop trying to give an identity to something that you know nothing about, so that your non-identity with the flesh can allow you to see the totality of you in the necessity for your transformation. So you are saying to the world: don't you understand? *A Course In Miracles* is teaching your own personal transformation from the very beginning to the end. All Jesus has ever taught is the necessity for you, individually, like unto what He is doing in association with you, to have your own personal experience. Nothing but that.

Nicodemus answered and said unto him, How can these things be? How can you be doing this? How are you able to do this? Art thou a master of Israel, and knowest not these things? said Jesus. (John 3:9-10) Are you a teacher and don't teach your own personal transformation? There is nothing in the Kabala, mystical Judaism, that did not make allowance for a manner by which you could come to know God. Obviously, it had to be rejected because the manner would have to be a cult or secret, since it was not contained in the association of what you would call the Sanhedrin, the Sadducees or the Scribe or even the political Zealot who said somehow we can build the Kingdom here on earth.

Art thou a master of Israel, and knowest not these things? Verily, verily, I say unto thee, We speak that we do know, and testify that we have seen; and ye receive not our witness. (John 3:10-11) Which is another way of saying that you won't even admit that we have had the experience. It's another way of saying: as long as you can separate Jesus from what He says, you can live in a reference where you will literally be nothing. Jesus says: what good does it do me to talk to you about my resurrection when you won't admit that I am resurrected? What good does it do me to tell you of my experiences when you deny me? What an astonishing demand for a reasonable self-observation!

We speak that we do know, and testify that we have seen; and ye receive not our witness. If I have told you earthly things, and ye believe not, how shall ye believe, if I tell you of heavenly things? (John 3:11-12) You can't know one without the other because they are the same. They will be part of your assertion or your admission or your surrender, to the experience of contact with God. This is the whole teaching of Jesus of Nazareth. You can't do this within your own association. Give everything away and come and follow me. The manner in which you come to know this is the admission that you don't know who you are, and can remember through being born again that you are perfect as God created you.

If I have told you earthly things, and ye believe not, how shall ye believe, if I tell you of heavenly things? (John 3:12) Be sure you understand the Great Cancel Out. What He says is that not only are you not willing to examine yourself, you are going to make up a physical association so that you can examine what you believe to be spiritual and find a correspondence in the so-called spiritual and physical, without the necessity to address your own association. What has happened here in this room today is that you are coming in and acknowledging the teachings of the resurrected man as the immediacy of the necessity for your own individual resurrection, without the fear of the consequences of immediacy. Nothing frightens you more than the simple acknowledgment that you are, at this moment, perfect as God created you. This is why you needed *A Course In Miracles*. You are no longer afraid of the physical immediacy of your own transformation. Are there energies all around telling you this? Of course.

If I told you earthly things, and ye believe not, how shall ye believe, if I tell you of heavenly things? (John 3:12) That is the separation of Jesus as the writer of the Course and as the Course. And no man hath ascended up to Heaven, but he that came down from Heaven, even the Son of man which is in Heaven. (John 3:13) This is the direct teaching of *A Course In Miracles,* isn't it. It teaches you are both in Heaven and on earth. If you think you are on earth, you will be on earth. If you think you are in Heaven, you will be in Heaven. But you can't be both in Heaven and on earth. If you think you are an earth-man, you must ascend to Heaven. But if you didn't come from Heaven in the first place, how would you know there is a Heaven? Obviously, the admission that you are separate, which must be included in with the entirety, is all this really teaches. What an amazing idea... . *even the Son of man, which is in Heaven.* Is the Son of man in Heaven? Sure. I thought you said the Son of God is in Heaven. He is! And the Son of man? He's in Heaven, too. You mean both the Son of man and the Son of God are in Heaven? Of course. Everything is in Heaven. Anything not in Heaven isn't real. But remember, if you bind yourself on earth, you've bound Heaven along with you.

See how confident John is in his mystical certainty? He needs to deal with the physical resurrection without presenting it directly when he says: And no man hath ascended up to Heaven, but he that came down from Heaven, even the Son of man which is in Heaven. And as Moses lifted up the serpent in the wilderness, even so must the Son of man be lifted up. (John 3:14) Watch out. Suddenly he's teaching about serpents, and Moses underwent the experience of the awakening of his body through the handling of his fear. It's amazing that man, primate, has an inherent fear of snakes. It's in man, it's in us. It's about the handling of the fear—the admission—without reducing it to some of these Protestant cults that handle snakes. It is an indication of the raising up, through the snake, through the ida and pingala, through the resurrection of man, through the caduceus of the experience.

As Moses lifted up the serpent in the wilderness, even so must the Son of man be lifted up: That whosoever believeth in him should not perish, but have everlasting life. (John 3:15) Believe in who? The man that's raised up! Jesus doesn't say: that's me. He says: whosoever believeth in his resurrection will be resurrected. If you believe in me you will be resurrected because I am resurrected and I am you. There's nothing that I have done or will ever do that you did not do and will have done and did. That's going to take the admission that you are the savior of the world. This is *A Course In Miracles.* This is going to require that you stand right there and say: this is my dream, I can have the experience of my resurrection. That's the last thing you want to do with Jesus: you want Him to either be a divine idol, or you want to reduce Him to your own manhood. The one thing you don't want to do is admit that He is you, because then you'd have to have your own experience of resurrection! He says that. In the Course He says: you constantly put me up so that you can idolize me and condemn me because of your inability to do it. Or you detract me and put me down to where you are and say: you must be using a method I can recognize.

Whosoever believeth in him should not perish –it's the whole Christian religion. That's what it says: whosoever believeth in him should not perish but have eternal life. It doesn't say "will not," it says "should not." What's the sense in doing it? You shouldn't do that. You should not perish.

For God so loved the world, that he gave his only begotten Son, that whosoever believeth in him should not perish, but have everlasting life. (John 3:16) That's the whole Christian idea. Did God give his son? Of course. God only gives his son. Do you recognize your sonship as the sonship of God? I hope so. God has given you eternal life. Identifying someone else as having eternal life isn't going to do you any good. Identification isn't what eternity is. Eternity is the acknowledgment of God.

For God sent not his Son into the world to condemn the world; but that the world through him might be saved. (John 3:17) That includes the condemnation of yourself in your associations and the recognition that in time you have come to know your own perfection through your transformation, through being born again.

He that believeth on him, the Son of God, is not condemned, but he that believeth not is condemned already –he's not going to be condemned later. If you are valuing mammon, you are denying God –you have already been condemned, you are dead. You need the

111

experience of the resurrection. Because he hath not believed in the name of the only begotten Son of God. (John 3:18) Remember just a moment ago we said that God has named you. He hasn't named someone else. Do you want to make this admission with me? I am talking to you about your own consciousness mind. Did God give me a name? Yes. What did He call me? My Only Begotten Son! What name do you want to assume? I'm not concerned about the name you assume. All I'm telling you that it is either perfect or it's nothing. You may be anything that you choose to be. But only under the direction of the totality of the necessity for your own transformation –not as to the method, but as to the certainty that you are whole and perfect as God created you.

And this is the condemnation, that light is come into the world, and men loved darkness rather than light, because their deeds were evil (John 3:19) or separate from God. Any comparison of the conceptual mind association will condemn you; anything that any human has manifested in your cause-and-effect relationship will condemn you to the result of your own physical and temporal association. This is the fundamental teaching of Christianity and *A Course In Miracles*.

For everyone that doeth evil (physical, body things) hateth the light. (John 3:20) This is why Jesus was rejected so emphatically. You say: well, I don't hate God. I just want Him to accept my separation, my association with sickness and pain, to authenticate His wholeness. No, no, no. There is nothing you feared more when you came into this church and sat down in this pew than your own physical resurrection. There is nothing you hated to admit more than that you had no value in your own identity. There is nothing that you hated more than the message that you are perfect as God created you. There is nothing you detested more than the idea that any temple would only be an establishment of death rather than life. Then you say: well, I'm practicing hating my dad, it says you have to hate your earthly father. Yes, it says that, and the next thing it says is: honor your father. Which does He mean? Yes!

... and men loved darkness rather than light, because their deeds were evil. For everyone that doeth evil hatest the light, neither cometh to the light, lest his deeds should be reproved. (John 3:20) This is nothing but the expression that you are guilty of your own associations and are afraid that God's going to punish you and condemn you.

But he that doeth truth cometh to the light, that his deeds may be made manifest, that they are wrought in God. (John 3:21) What an interesting idea that you can "do truth." A man who "doeth truth" –a man who extends the certainty of his own association. In that sense, the miracle is a doing of the truth of what you are. Your declaration: I am perfect as God created me says: I will do as I am directed. I will relinquish the world. I will give it up. I cannot serve God and mammon. I don't want this association! That is what "doing truth" is. Doing truth is denying the world. This is *A Course In Miracles* –you will do truth because you are truth, if you will deny the necessity of your own association. That's being born again! What you are saying is, that if I don't bring my fear with me, each moment I am going to be classified as a Born-Again Christian. What do you teach at the New Christian Church? We teach that you've got to be born again, and I'm being born again. When are you being born again. NOW. Really? When is the Second Coming? NOW. But, he that doeth truth cometh to the light, that his deeds may be made manifest, that they are wrought in God. That's John.

But whosoever drinketh of the water that I shall give him shall never thirst; but the water that I shall give him shall be in him a well of water springing up into everlasting life. (John 4:14) How come he uses water so much? The two things that occur the most in efforts to express this are light and water. Water. Why? Water is an explosion. Did you know that? Any physicist will tell you that it is a tremendous energy; it then becomes a residual, or a potential, for the use of the two parts of hydrogen and one part of oxygen (H_2O). How come you've got two hydrogens and one oxygen? It is an explosion. Then you can take the water and walk on it, or use the water to change your mind in order to do this. That's one thing you can't do with nitrogen, that's for sure. Nitrogen is described as one of the most explosive things around. But compared to the explosion of hydrogen and oxygen, nitrogen is nothing. You're just exploding from your nitrogen fixation to a new association into the kingdom of God!

John's lovely. He writes all this stuff. He's an old guy by now. He's telling a story of himself. You'll notice in John, if you sometime will look at the Book, John doesn't deal with Jesus' lineage at all.

There's nothing in John that says: Jesus descended from Moses. It's not there. He starts out immediately by saying: In the beginning there was perfection and Jesus manifested. That's all he says. In that sense, you do make some progress. How much progress do you want to make? Do you prefer to be Matthew, or Levi, who teaches Pharisaically the necessity for the Jew to come to Christ. It's his whole teaching. Mark, who is a follower of Peter, is very pithy and describes the descendants of Jesus from Adam rather than from Moses. This is the progress from the Jew to the totality. So Mark says "straight away" fifteen times. Mark will say "straight away" - this will occur *now*. Luke tells a great story. Only in Luke do we get the Christmas story with the wisemen. He has a necessity to tell a story to you about your association with the divine. By the time you get to John it's very mystical. He's teaching you directly in Revelations, which is part of the same gospel, of the necessity for your transformation.

So this is the Bible class, talking about what Jesus says and what He says you are. You have come to know what you are through transformation and your resurrection of your spatial/temporal association. Is it okay for me to transfigurate? Is it all right if I have this experience? You'll have to tell me. Is it all right with you? The only thing that could possibly deny you the experience would be you in your determination of what you want to do in your own association. If you want to say: my home awaits me, I'm going home, that's all right with me. If you want to leave here, go ahead. How come you came back so quickly? I watch you guys go through your transformation, and then I see you back here. Are you appearing behind closed doors? If you want, you can depart the world right now. There you are. How did it go? I can't speak of that. But I can speak of the certainty that is involved with what I know I am.

This is the whole teaching of Jesus and *A Course In Miracles*. It says the resurrection is going on all the time. You were only here for a moment, right? Is that so? When is that moment? Now. Yes, but you are still here. I see you sitting in that pew. Really?

If I so choose, I can depart this world entirely. It is not death which makes this possible, but it is change of mind about the purpose of the world. Obviously, if the purpose of the Academy is to teach you to undergo the transformation, nothing will stop you from doing that, *if* that is your purpose. What could possibly stop you, if you thought you were separated, from coming home and being as God created you? The answer, obviously, is nothing. *If I believe it has a value as I see it now, so will it remain for me. But, if I see no value in the world as I behold it, nothing that I want to keep as mine or search for as a goal, it will depart from me.* Why does that sound like Jesus of Nazareth? You can't do both. You are either going to be whole as God created you, or you are going to be whole as God created you. Spoken like an awakened mind. *For I have not sought for illusions to replace the truth.* (Lesson 226)

This is our prayer as you came in the door, and this is our Sunday school prayer: *Father, it is today that I am free, because my will is Yours. I thought to make another will. Yet nothing that I thought apart from You exists.* This world does not exist because it is not a part of God. Are you going to be able to teach that? This world does not exist because it is not a part of God. There is no such thing as this. There is no such thing as that mind that studies this. *And I am free because I was mistaken...* I am free because I thought I was separated from God, but it wasn't true, and I'm glad to know that I'm not actually separated, so I don't have to participate in this world. But, if I do participate in it, I'm going to get the results of my own participation. Boy, is that Pharisaical: I can come to God. What's the difference in it? We're directing you to your personal salvation. You must be born again. *And I am free because I was mistaken, and did not affect my own reality at all by my illusions. Now I give them up, and lay them down before the feet of truth, to be removed forever from my mind.* Notice it doesn't say that I'm going to remove them. I'm going to lay them down. I'm not going to study like Nicodemus and ask: How the hell did you do that? How did you come to know that? What method did you use to come to know to work these miracles? Jesus said: I didn't use any method at all. I recognized who I had to be and, in that, everyone was healed, because I was the cause of their sickness. You change your mind and they are healed. You may go through a period, and it may start any minute, that you will begin to demonstrate miraculous healing. The result of that will be a very high range of Pharisee, where the associations will remain separate from you and demand to know in private how you were able to do that. Your whole attention to them must be then to their own personal resurrection. If you are hell-bent on describing your own awakening in relationship with other associations, you are going to be trapped in it. You will be trapped as a Pharisee with the admission of the resurrection, but not the necessity for the individual transformation. *This is my holy instant of release. Father, I know my will is one with Yours. And so today we find our glad return to Heaven, which we never really left. The Son of God this day lays down his dreams. The Son of God this day comes home again, released from sin and clad in holiness, with his right mind restored to him at last.* (Lesson 227)

Are you clad in holiness? Have you put on the Christ body? Have you taken the body of the limitations of your own apparent association in darkness and clad yourself in light? All the descriptions of resurrection include figures of light. Can they be misidentified or identified as angels? Sure. In the resurrection there's different ways to handle it. Matthew has an angel roll the stone back, then the guards can fall asleep because, obviously, they can't see it. Mark had a young man clothed in white, sitting on the right side in the sepulcher. By the time it gets to John, he has two angels sitting at the head and feet, and everybody goes in and sees that He is gone. The physical resurrection of the man is acknowledged.

There are a lot of stories coming out about angels, aren't there –how the angels are all around. Are the angels all around? Sure. They're just factorings of your own thought-mind. If you give specific attention to the holy association of yourself to the relief from that particular predicament based on the openness of your determination to come to God, the angels will always be there. How about evil angels, will they help you do evil? You bet. The question will always be, as I just read you: What's It For? What is the purpose for which you are doing this? How are you using, in your genetic code, the relation between your RNA and your DNA? The activation of your cellular memories are undergoing continuing reassociations of light based on what you call enzymes. Angels are enzymes; they are communicators within the DNA and RNA of a method of changing you altogether. Obviously, angels are communicators. They are always giving you messages."He's not here, He went home. He will meet you over there." He hasn't left you; He's in a later time association. Go there and He will teach you a new time. Why? He's resurrected. Where did He go? Right back to where you started from. You were going to go back to fishing. That's all you're really doing. You go back to where you are, so that you can see where you are is home with God.

Is it okay that you are the light of the world? You're going to be the light of the world, whether it's okay with you or not. At least you have sufficient attention directing you to see that you are the cause of this, and that the outcome can be determined, and was determined, by the transformation of your mind. But if that's true, you aren't teaching time at all. Actually what Jesus says to his most beloved, John, is that if you believe me, you will never die. He's obviously talking in temporal associations, where there is a necessity to teach the kingdom. Having to teach the kingdom is obviously a reduction, this is *A Course In Miracles*. Having to teach forgiveness, which is a Peter-ism, is a reduction of the necessity for the admission of the perfection of the association. There's no need for forgiveness in perfection.

He that loveth his life shall lose it; and he who hateth his life in this world shall keep it unto life eternal. (John 12:25) Holy mackerel. And whither I go ye know, and the way ye know. (John 14:4) Wow. Where I'm going you know perfectly well. What an amazing idea. Now let's look right at the end where John makes his own confession.

This is now the third time that Jesus shewed Himself to his disciples, after that he was risen from the dead. So when they had dined, Jesus said to Simon Peter, Simon, son of Jonas (son of man), lovest thou me more than these? He saith, Yea, Lord; thou knowest that I love thee. He saith unto him, Feed my lambs. (John 21:14) The problem is that Jesus knows that Peter loves Him, but Peter doesn't know, because the love of Peter for Jesus is actually the love of Peter for Peter. This is the fact of the matter. So Jesus keeps saying to him that there is a discipline contained in the totality of love rather than the determination to serve the idol of an apparently resurrected man. So He says, Simon, son of Jonas, lovest thou me more than these? He saith, Yea, Lord; thou knowest that I love thee. He saith unto him, Feed my lambs. Take my message and declare it to be true of me even if you can't see it in yourself. That's what He says. Then He does it again.

He saith to him again the second time, Simon, son of Jonas, lovest thou me? He saith unto him, Yea, Lord; thou knowest that I love thee. He saith unto him, Feed my sheep. (John 21:16) Carry my message. Then He says it to him another time.

He saith unto him the third time, Simon, son of Jonas, lovest thou me? Peter was grieved because he said unto him the third time, Lovest thou me? And he said unto him, Lord, thou knowest all things; thou knowest that I love thee. (John 21:17) No, that's not the way it works. It was necessary that *Peter* knowest all things. He does it three times, because Peter, obviously, has denied Him three times. Peter has recognized his own guilt and is determined to no longer deny Jesus, but to retain the guilt of the necessity to atone for what he did in the denial. That's exactly what Peter does, even to being crucified upside down —at the very end, Peter is determined that he has been the messenger of Jesus, and to prove it, he would never be crucified like his savior. Why not? What kind of a statement is it to be crucified upside down, if it isn't somewhere an establishment determination to authenticate a causation for the perfection of himself? That's the way it works.

Jesus saith unto him, Feed my sheep. Verily, verily, I say unto thee, When thou wast young, thou girdedst thyself, and walkedst whither thou wouldest; but when thou shalt be old, thou shalt stretch forth thy hands, and another shall gird thee, and carry thee whither thou wouldest not. (John 21:18) It's another statement that even though you're in a body and you think you're going to die, at least let the message of your own associations accumulate so that the ancient times, or the holy instances being experienced, can become a part of this temporal association. That was the requirement for the establishment of the church on earth in the first place, otherwise why would you need it?

This spake he, signifying by what death he should glorify God. And when he had spoken this, he saith unto him, Follow me. Then Peter, turning about, seeth the disciple whom Jesus loved following. (John 21:19) Here comes John. Actually, he's about to follow Jesus right into Heaven. Jesus turns around and says: Follow me. John says: Yep. He's already instructed Peter to stay here and teach his associations. Peter says: what the heck is going on here?

Then Peter, turning about, seeth the disciple whom Jesus loved following; which also leaned on his breast at supper, and said, Lord, which is he that betrayeth thee? (John 21:20) Peter didn't like that. Peter did not like that John, when Jesus said that somebody is going to betray me, asked if it was going to be me. Because John had a totality of the acknowledgment of his own sinfulness, not in relation to salvation. Peter said: No, it will never be me. The moment he said: no, it will never be me, Jesus said: yes it will. The statement "it will never be me" is the denial of his own perfection. So Peter says to John: how dare you tell me you can follow Jesus right out of here; or better, if you don't follow Him, Jesus is going to acknowledge to you that He is always with you, and therefore you cannot die. That's what this will say. Obviously, somewhere Jesus is expressing a favor for John. He says: John's my most beloved one. Why? John can see Him in the totality of their association with each other. John is not concerned about what Jesus was before at all; only in the certainty of the relevance of the immediate transformation of his mind. Jesus just got through giving instructions to Peter. He's saying to Peter: teach what I am. The minimum the Course says in order to get this is that you've got to teach it. You can't get it without making a declaration. That's the requirement.

Then Peter, turning about, seeth the disciple whom Jesus loved following; which also leaned on his breast at supper, and said, Lord, which is he that betrayeth thee? Peter seeing him saith to Jesus, Lord, what shall this man do? (John 21:21) He's very nervous about this fellow. How come you didn't tell him to feed the sheep? Obviously, Jesus is in recognition with John of what you guys are recognizing in each other. You guys are obviously recognizing in each other the single purpose of your union through the transformation of your body. Never did I say to you: I want you to go out and establish some things and begin to teach. I did not say that to you. You have become that association with me. Nowhere, when you came into this room, did I say: let's all go out and you teach this Pharisaically; teach in the possibility of the association of your own mind, but only my direct concern with you in our love for each other and for God.

Peter seeing him saith to Jesus, Lord, what shall this man do? Jesus saith unto him, If I will that he tarry till I come, what is that to thee? (John 21:22) What He actually says is John is going to stay with me all the time. John will be with me as I come and go in this teaching.

I'm going to teach you from time to tarry for a moment here in the recognition of my resurrection in the entirety of your teaching –that's *A Course In Miracles.* Isn't that fun? You are having that experience. He understands that the guys are saying that John can't die. John is also aware that he can't die; but he's also aware of the entirety of the continuum in the reference to life and death, and He does not want Peter not to practice the continuation. So He says it rather subtly.

Then went this saying abroad among the brethren, that that disciple (John) should not die; yet Jesus said not unto him, He shall not die –but that he could not die –but, If I will that he tarry till I come, what is that to thee? (John 21:23) That is literally a denial of death. No matter how it would be demonstrated here, you, as a follower of Jesus, have the certainty in your mind of the resurrection, that you are the resurrection and the light. If you tarry here for a moment, as the Course would teach, let that teaching of your resurrection emanate through the Peter-ism of the denial of God and influence the decision that has already been made.

This is the disciple which testifieth of these things, and wrote these things: and we know that his testimony is true. (He's talking about himself.) And there are also many other things which Jesus did, and which, if they should be written every one, I suppose that even the world itself could not contain the books that should be written. (John 21:24-25) So I'm not going to try to do it anymore. I'm going to tell you that you aren't "man" –there's no such thing as man. It was a transient step through time. This is what John, the same John who wrote the synoptic gospel, wrote in Revelations: he had the experience that Heaven and earth would pass away and be no more, and that man would become a whole new thing. There's some good stuff in here. The trick is to start from the assumption of the necessity of your own resurrection, and then it will be very apparent to you.

This is the workbook: *Now is the time of prophecy fulfilled, for now we cannot fail.* It is the prayer book (lessons 221-365). In the admission that you cannot fail is the expression of yourself coming into the immediacy of the fear that you expressed before, and walking in this door and simply saying: I am undergoing a physical resurrection. I need not be afraid.

Fear is not justified in any form. Fear not! You are celebrating "fear not," for behold, I bring you good tidings of great joy. For unto you is born this day, in the city of David, the savior who is Christ the Lord. And this shall be a sign unto you: you shall find the babe wrapped in swaddling clothes, lying in the manger. (Luke 2:10-12) The Christ is being born in you? Yes! Are the wisemen all going to come? Luke says the wisemen come.

Fear is deception. It attests that you have seen yourself as you could never be, and therefore look upon a world which is impossible. Since you have seen yourself as fearful, you must look on a fearful world, because this world is a reflection of your thoughts. I'm teaching *A Course In Miracles* here. I'm just curious to see why you keep insisting that I give some sort of direction to the other associations –what do I care? What do I care how anyone comes to know this? I'm telling you this is all a construction of your own mind. If you undergo the experience, the world will be over and gone. People will say: I want to know how you came to know that. It's none of your business; it's God's business, not yours. Let it be God's business, Pharisee. Know ye not that you must be born again? It has to happen to you. Go handle some snakes. Go have some fearful experiences so you can stay in the fear of what you are, in the sense that you have seen yourself as you can never be, and therefore look upon a world that is impossible. Are you ready: Not one thing in this world is true. Including the statement: Not one thing in this world is true. I'm saying this world is not true, including this, that's *A Course In Miracles* –including your need to know that's true, because it's going to be true whether you know it or not. Now you're going to get the Pharisees that are really going to want to know how you know this: Know ye not that you must be born again?

Now you're going to teach the Course. All you're going to teach them is what it says. It says you are the cause of this. Do not underestimate the capacity of the Pharisaical mind. It has progressed to the determination that it is possible, without the admission that it is only possible through them. That's how they keep it off. They've escaped the establishment, at least sufficiently to allow that man is progressing to the truth, but not the necessity of the admission of their own salvation. Not one thing in this world is true. It does not matter what the form in which it may appear. It witnesses but to your own illusions of yourself. Let us not be deceived today. We are the Sons of God. There is no fear in us, for we are each a part of Love Itself. *How foolish are our fears! Would You allow Your Son to suffer? Give us faith today to recognize Your Son, and set him free. Let us forgive him in Your Name, that we may understand his holiness, and feel the love for him which is Your Own as well.* (Lesson 240)

I came here to testify to you that there is no way I'm going to give you an identity in your own condition of yourself. If you are tempted to believe that something here is true, I am going to say: no, that is not so. I'm going to practice *A Course In Miracles*. I'm going to see the perfection through the release of the necessity to defend my identity.

This is a lovely book (lessons 221-365 of *A Course In Miracles*). What is the Real World? What is the Second Coming? What is the Last Judgment? It's all in here.

I seek a future different from the past. Virtually all of you are in this position. Never mind the old —whatever the future is, it's not going to be like this. *From new perception of the world there comes a future very different from the past. The future now is recognized as but an extension of the present.* You see how easy it is. You come to this level of time, you are in a present condition, and you begin to extend it, without the necessity of the old identification —without the need to hold onto that. *Past mistakes can cast no shadows on it, so that fear has lost its idols and its images, and being formless, it has no effects. Death will not claim the future now, for life is now its goal, and all the needed means are happily provided.* I don't know if you guys really understand what most of you sitting in this room really are —through your denial of death, you are alive! Through your denial of the past, you have come to this place in space/time. Most of you in this room would have no more idea of wanting to be a human being; now you don't know what the outcome of this is going to be. All you had to know is that the outcome is not going to be death. Since it can't be death, it must be eternity. What have you lost? Your fear of physical resurrection. Death will not claim the future now, for life is now its goal and all the needed means are happily provided. *Who can grieve or suffer when the present has been freed, extending its security and peace into a quiet future filled with joy? Father, we were mistaken in the past, and choose to use the present to be free. Now do we leave the future in Your Hands, leaving behind our past mistakes, and sure that You will keep Your present promises, and guide the future in your holy light.* (Lesson 314)

This is for you alone: All power is given unto you, individually, in Heaven and in earth. There is nothing you cannot do. Father, *I have a special place to fill; a role for me alone.* Obviously, how would you not have a role —you've given yourself a role of sickness and pain —you must have a role of salvation. Has the roll been called up yonder? When the roll is called, will you be there? When the roll is called, you are there. That's what this says. You are the dreamer of the dream. *Salvation waits until I take this part as what I choose to do. Until I make this choice, I am the slave of time and human destiny.* All humanity is destined to die, to turn back in on itself, to be trapped in its own beginning and its own end. I must change my mind in order that the world can be changed, and that human destiny can be changed, the destiny of death can be changed. To what? The destiny of Life! *But, when I willingly and gladly go the way my Father's plan appointed me to go, then will I recognize salvation is already here, already given all my brothers and already mine as well. Father, Your way is what I choose today. Where it would lead me do I choose to go; what it would have me do I choose to do. Your way is certain, and the end secure. The memory of You awaits me there. And all my sorrows end in Your embrace, which You have promised to Your Son, who thought mistakenly that he had wandered from the sure protection of Your loving Arms.* (Lesson 317)

In me, God's holy Son, are reconciled all parts of Heaven's plan to save the world. It's not that God didn't have separate parts, but in each separate part was the totality of what I am. *What could conflict, when all the parts have but one purpose and one aim? How could there be a single part that stands alone, or one that's more or less important than the rest? I am the means by which God's Son is saved, because salvation's purpose is to find the sinlessness that God has placed in me. I was created as the thing I seek.* I am not the thing you seek, you are! It's the whole teaching. You can direct me and assemble me and do anything you want with me. I am not the thing you seek. If I were, you would have already found me. That's the fact of the matter. The salvation I offer you is only yours. *I was created as the thing I seek. I am the goal the world is searching for.* Can you hear that? The one you are searching for is me; because all I'm going to tell you is that you are perfect as God created you and you can come home and be with God. Obviously, you don't want to find me. All you are really saying now is: yes, I really want to find you. Can you stand up and say: I was created as the thing I think –that is the certainty that you are the cause of this –followed by: I am the goal the world is searching for. Notice it does not say: I am the savior the world is searching for. I am the *goal,* I am what you are looking for in the entirety of you. Isn't that nice. *I am God's Son, His one eternal Love. I am salvation's means and end as well.* Because the means and the end are together. Every time I make a declaration of the wholeness of my mind, I am whole. Every time I come into my own associations with myself, I am nothing. *Let me today, my Father, take the role You offer me in Your request that I accept Atonement for myself. For thus does what is thereby reconciled in me become as surely reconciled to You.* (Lesson 318)

What an amazing idea. The whole teaching is God needs you as much as you need Him. He can't get along without you. There's no Heaven without you. You're just waking up from a dream. Is that okay with you? Is that the fun you are having? All of these illusions of attack and defense were never true. Thank you for allowing me to teach this. Are you coming to know that this is true? It is but myself that I attack. There is no conflict. My will is yours. This is lovely. What is the last judgment? God himself will take the last step. So all of my ideas of trying to teach it outside myself are not going to stop this.

My Self is ruler of the universe. It is impossible that anything should come to me unbidden by myself. Even in this world, it is I who rule my destiny. What happens is what I desire. What does not occur is what I do not want to happen. I can depart this world right now simply by desiring it. But I must desire it in its entirety, or my mind will be split to be in the association of time or eternity. That's where I find myself. But this world is about to end, isn't it? What happens is what I desire. *What does not occur is what I do not want to happen. This must I accept.* I must accept it. I don't have to believe it. I must accept it as true that I am the entirety of the cause, be it painful, sick and dead or alive and whole. The acceptance of that will lead you directly to the truth of you, very simply because it is true that you are the cause of this. *For thus am I led past this world to my creations, children of my will, in Heaven where my holy Self abides with them and Him Who has created me. You are the Self Whom You created Son, creating like Yourself and one with You. My Self, Which rules the universe, is but Your Will in perfect union with my own, which can but offer glad assent to Yours, that it may be extended to Itself.* (Lesson 253)

There's no earth without you. There's no hell without you. There's no happiness without you. There's no sickness or pain without you. There's no death without you. There's no life without you. Without you there is nothing. But since you cannot be nothing, you must be everything. As everything, you allow yourself to be you in the entirety of your own mind and will not attempt to identify yourself in the separation. Do you understand me? That's our catechism for today. This is a church, isn't it? Do you come here to communicate? What's astonishing is that a lot of you are staying here at all. Listen, guys, this is not a real place. The provisions you have given yourself in spatial references are just momentary determinations of yours to abide here for a moment. Thank you. Because no one in their right mind would stay here any longer than necessary. I'm not concerned what your necessity is, nor need I be, if you have seen the light; if you know you are perfect as God created you. Obviously, no one here knows that. How can they know it? You have just discovered it. Now you have a choice of being gone altogether or teaching what you have come to know through your own transformation. Obviously, if you are gone altogether, we can't give you a teaching assignment. So, somewhere, as John would teach, we are prevailing on you to use this resurrection energy to afford the second coming –why not?

This is your healing center, isn't it. What are you going to do with sick people that come to you? You're going to tell them that only transformation heals. You're going to tell them that they are cured by the change of your mind. You are going to show them through the energy of your love that they are perfect. It's not really difficult to do. In fact, it's the simplest thing in the world to do. The difficulty has been your need to stay separate –that's where all your grievances come from. You put up a real good battle to stay separate from God; but it's only in your own mind.

So I like your New Christian Church of Full Endeavor. It's teaching born again. It's teaching second coming. It's teaching that Christ has risen as the perfect son of God and is in Heaven, and has invited you there. Where is the objection? It's to the personal transformation of the individual. That he is the cause of it is where the objection will occur. It would have to. Why? Because of fear. He's afraid he's the cause of cancer. There's nothing to be afraid of, is there? You're not afraid, are you? I was always not afraid, because I don't let myself happen to what's happening. Instead I asked them how they did it. By asking how they did it, I can keep from having the experience myself –I can write letters to the Academy and say: what are you doing to bring this about? I don't have to have my own experience.

Are you the only one left here? Is that true? Can you hear this? I came specifically to get you. But as soon as you came, you discovered that all those you had previously denied and attacked were actually a part of your mind, so they're coming along with you. How could they not? You offered them the totality of your own mind. It's getting pretty crowded. We're going to transfer a bunch of you over to the other side, then you can invite everyone else out. That will be the end of this association. You're not saying to the guy next to you: what the hell is going on here? You're saying: follow me, I'm going to go and see what that is. I'm not going to tarry here to try and decide what to do. I've been told exactly what I'm to do. I'm supposed to give up the world and come to God. At least, I can't say I wasn't told. That's what we're trying to do.

Are you happy to hear there is no world? Isn't that nice to know that this world is not true, that this is not a part of God, that there is no such thing as loneliness and sickness and death, and you can't get old and you can't die. Aren't you happy to know that? You'll have to answer your own questions. I don't know where you are in relationship to yourself. One thing for sure, if you want this world to be true, it will be true for you. Initially, you may be happy to hear this, and then become fearful. You've been forced into an association with your own mind. You must be born again yourself. Know ye not that *you* must have the experience, not as telling the story about someone else. The story is you. You are the dreamer of the dream. You must have the experience. Aren't you glad? What about the rest of the world? What world? There is no world without you. If you want to save your loved ones, take them home to Heaven with you. Stop denying them and killing them in your own associations. They await your salvation. You are the one that has determined that they get sick and die. They depend on you.

If your name is on the roll, raise your hand. I have no reason to doubt you whatsoever. And if you get up to the gate and they can't find your name, keep on walking. The guy searching for your name doesn't know anything more about it than you do. Your name is on there. Nobody can tell you that you can't go in. Don't fall into Peter-ism, who is guarding the gate. Peter is time. Peter is going to seek to know how you came separately to identify him, rather than simply recognizing the Christ who is coming up to his gate. If Peter, the gatekeeper, recognizes the Christ, he'll say: holy mackerel, is that you? Christ will say: Peter, it's me.

And Peter will walk right through his own door. Peter will turn around and follow you right out! Why wouldn't he? There's no one determining who's coming to the door but your own Peter-ism. Well, we've been teaching this, and I want to see if you've really fulfilled the requirements. You say: I have, I'm going home. He'll immediately stand aside for you. Whether he's determined to continue to remain this side of the Borderland, I have no idea, but certainly you've opened up the gates of Heaven. The more of you that come, the wider the gate has become. Now you are inviting everyone in the association. Are there enough Peters to stand and deny you? You look at them and see how small they are, they can't stop you. They are impotent to affect you in the slightest. When your minds are open, it's very joyous, isn't it? Finally you see that the whole thing is a joke! Salvation is the recognition that this whole thing is a joke. Jesus will say in the Course that it is a joke to think that you could actually be separate from God, that you could suffer sickness and pain. It's a joke, deserving to be laughed at. Hopefully, that's what you are doing.

When someone says: stay here and die. You say: what the hell are you talking about? Why would I want to do that? Why would I want to be a human being? Why would I want to be like you? You're laughable.

You're ridiculous. You're shaking your fist at the whole universe and nobody cares. You're battling your own self in your own mind. You are able to laugh even though the joke was on you. Now you can laugh at the joke being on you. You're not the butt of the joke; you are the joke. It's kind of a practical joke. You say: I wish you hadn't done that, it scared the hell out of me. I didn't mean to. Sorry. It was a mistake. I thought you would know instantly that it wasn't real. But, you took it very seriously. If you can't forgive me for the joke, you can't get out of here. If you are going to hold me to it and not admit that it's a joke, I can't stop you from blaming me for the cause. That's what forgiveness is. Into the universe crept a tiny mad idea, and you forgot to laugh. I don't blame you, this isn't very funny. Look at this place. Look at this place!

Thank you for Bible study. We learned about Nicodemus. Know ye not that you must be born again? Well, I know that's talked about. I know *A Course In Miracles* teaches it. But, let's look conceptually at what the Course teaches. **It teaches, DON'T look conceptually at what it teaches.** Admit what it says and come home! How could anyone possibly be reading this and not understand it? But that's exactly what Jesus says to Nicodemus: How can you not know that? The entire teaching is personal transformation. There is nothing in Christianity except personal transformation.

CHAPTER EIGHT

The Kingdom of Heaven

You are using the reasonable power of your mind in application to determine the outcome, the efficacy, of a remedy in regard to a disease that is a conceptual association of your objective reality. That is the condition of conceptual mind. I don't want you to get out of your concepts. How could you get out of them? Somewhere you have to change your own mind in association with yourself about the outcome that you are getting as a result of your concepts. All you have really discovered is that the outcome of the limited association, based on an old reference, couldn't have any meaning. That discovery included your not wanting to give it meaning, very simply because you were getting the outcome of the concepts of your own mind. Somewhere you said: that's silly. The condition of a human being doesn't make any sense, because he is admitting that he is getting the outcome of the concepts of his own mind without questioning why or for what purpose he would get an outcome of himself. What's the sense in it?

The Kingdom of God is nothing but the inclusive precept of an idea that mind will be mind, and that any of your concepts can be included in with it. That's the Kingdom of God. Why do you have to tell the story of the Kingdom of God as a parable? There's no other way you can do it, because the Kingdom of God is not a description of objective reality. When I asked my mom, What's the Kingdom of Heaven? She said, "Well, gold flows in the street, and there are angels that hover around." That's an objective definition of it. Obviously I could say I am not in that Kingdom. I am in this Kingdom. How can I get to that Kingdom? It's not possible. If I separate myself from the Kingdom, and give it a definition of my objective association, it would be impossible for me to get there. I have separated myself from my own mind. I am comparing heaven and hell separate from what I am.

Once I get you in your own mind, and I can keep you from conceptualizing in objective reality, and comparing it with associations, what experience will you begin to have? A new joyous you! This is the whole Workbook. There is nothing outside of you. The wholeness that you are feeling is an expression of your association with universal mind. One thing for sure, there is no way you are teaching a human being to escape his concepts and the idea of comparison of one with the other. You are telling him that's impossible. Reality must be based on the fundamental premise of the possibility of the totality. I'll tell you any story you want to hear. Who cares? The effect of the totality of your mind is going to be in relationship with every single thing you do. The Kingdom of God is like to a lost colony. I'll give you parables. But notice I am always telling you about a relationship between the separation and reality. It is impossible that I not do that because that is what you are. There is no comparison and no association between this hell –this pain, this death, this loneliness, this loss, this attack on God –and the beautiful living universal mind of God.

As Jesus says: if I can get you to accept the premise that your condition of temporal relationship is an attack on God, directly and fully; that your need to die is literally a denial and an attack on God, you can progress in this very rapidly. Why? You become inclusive in your own sin. And sin won't make any sense to you, because by its inclusiveness you will see that you are combating something that must be contained within your own association. That's true! It's always going on. All saviors of the world are attempting to get you to look at the totality of your own association by entering, in your mind, into a relationship between the Son which is you, and God which is everything. That's the whole purpose of this. You must do it in your own mind. There is no other way. Now the fact of the matter is, what I am threatening you with, your own sickness, pain and death, is nothing compared to Jesus of Nazareth. The teachings of Jesus of

Nazareth, *A Course In Miracles*, have no sympathy at all for pain and death. Your salvation literally depends on me not allowing you your conceptual associations. Somewhere you believe that contained within your concepts will be a solution to the problem of who you are. That's absurd. You are perfect and whole as God created you.

So we tell stories. Would you like the one about the aliens that keep landing here and you keep covering them up? Is there one about an invitation to you to come home and celebrate your home coming? Are those the parables of Jesus? What does He say? He says the Kingdom of God is like to... and then He tells you a story. I have no concern about the story that you tell. I'm telling you that if you don't listen to the story that I'm offering you in its entirety, you will get the result of the limitation of your mind in the determination to accept our previous associations with each other, rather than letting yourself be whole in your own mind. The Kingdom of God is the relationship of Tom Sawyer, Huck Finn –anything –who cares. For goodness sake, what is the purpose in your own mind of the story you tell? Show me any human being, and I'll show you someone in his own Kingdom. He is the definition of himself in the determination of the outcome he wants with what he is in his own mind.

Not only is the human mind nuts, but a human being considers existence as being crazy. If he would look at it, he would see that he has lost control of everything in his association. No matter what he does, his determination is based on predications of results he wants in his own mind that are changing all the time. What is his problem? He has a fundamental flaw in his premise. His premise is that he must exist in this association rather than the simple admission of a premise of a whole mind. That's as simple as it gets. I won't tell you about St. Paul and everyone else who has told you this. I am telling you this as a fact of your own mind. The expansion of your association in correspondence with yourself, the miracle that has occurred with you, is very simply the need not to defend the old cause and effect relationships of your mind. I guarantee you that once you defend it, that old premise will become the premise from which you think. That will then become a form, and constrict you within your own mind. It's totally senseless. It has no basis, on any reasonable admission, that would withstand any light of examination. Hopefully, you are understanding that *A Course*

In Miracles is a course in the reasonableness of singular, universal mind. I'm not taking your premises away from you. I'm just asking you to look at the premises on which your existence has been based to determine what it is in your own association. You mean if I change my mind the world will really change? I mean that the world is your mind. I mean that the whole universe is your mind. I'm saying, story after story, that you are that!

How did this come about in your new minds? How are you now able to see with clarity that you are whole with God? You simply made the admission that God was God. It was simpler than you wanted to admit. You stopped being the authority of your own conceptual mind in order to die. How reasonable does this world still seem to you? As reasonable as the result you are determined to get without looking at the obvious outcome, death. The real insanity is the conceptual mind, first of all, accepts the outcome that appears to be inevitable –he gives away his own causation, and secondly, he then lives by not looking at the absurdity of that association. The idea that the universe is a premise of my mind of the totality of eternal life is very exciting to me. All I needed was so-called progress within my own apparent chaotic association, to the determination that I couldn't solve the problem that I was obviously facing within the context of what appeared to be the solution to it. It's not solvable. That's all it took. Reasonably, any problem that leads to sickness and death could not be solved, because the problem of sickness and death is what it is. The whole teaching that I have told you is: your Kingdom is not of this world. You have examined the precepts of existence being terminal which the world is based on, and have seen that it is senseless.

Just for the fun of it, I'll tell you the story of Matthew 22. It is exactly the same story that I've been telling you about the original invitation that you rejected and killed the Christ, or that was a screw up of communication within the association. You were prepared within your own mind to hear this. The invitation to come to God was extended to this expeditionary force. You received an invitation to come on home and be reunited with God. But there was a break in communication and you rejected it. Not only that, but your leaders failed you; those who were trained best through an observation of the orders they had read failed you because the orders were faulty. When

Jesus was faced with this, He would say: the Kingdom of God is like to... All of the stories will pertain to the offer of God and your rejection of it, or that you have no control over what God is doing, and/or the manner in which you can come to know it by giving everything away and coming to God. There would be no other stories but that.

And Jesus answered and spake unto them again by parables, and said... Why is Jesus answering them? Because they're always asking questions. Every time I say to you: you are perfect as God created you, you keep asking me questions about it. You have to have a story about how it happened. You *are* a story about how it happened. There was a mistake. It's a great story: *The Kingdom of Heaven is like unto a certain king, which made a marriage for his son*. That's nothing but the certainty of God expressing His determination to give you, His son, the total creative power that He is. He made a marriage for you. What's He going to unite him with? All of his potential. He is going to unite him with everything that he is.

And sent forth his servants to call them that were bidden to the wedding: and they would not come. (Matthew 22:1-3) Why wouldn't they come? They're too busy living in their own existent associations. He said to them, "Come and share the feast of the totality," and they wouldn't come. So there is no question that the invitation has been issued by God. This is the idea of God, or the invention in the mind that there is a perfect association; and the admission that you, as a human being, are rejecting the call of God. You'd have to be. Why? You know about it. I didn't invent God for you; you invented Him –you invented the solution. If you invented the solution, why not utilize it?

Again, he sent forth other servants, saying, Tell them which are bidden, Behold, I have prepared my dinner, my oxen and my fatlings are killed, and all things are ready: come unto the marriage. (Matthew 22:4) What he did was allow them the abundance of their own mind in the sharing of God. He had to give them a definition of what abundance was in the totality of the association, because they were trapped in the necessity of themselves. So he says, "At least come together with me and enjoy the real purpose in life, and my happiness, which is the marriage of my son. Okay, bring yourselves, I'll prepare the meal, I have another purpose I want to offer you." That's what we used to do in the Missions –get them in and feed them and get them to listen. Usually we'd give them the prayer first and then let them eat. If you fed them first, they'd leave.

... he sent forth other servants, saying, Tell them which are bidden... Only those which are bidden. Those that somewhere in the association are aware of that possibility of doing it, and can be aware that they are the deniers of it. But what did they do? They made light of it. They said: I'm getting along all right.

But they made light of it, and went their ways, one to his farm, another to his merchandise. And the remnant took his servants, and entreated them spitefully, and slew them. But when the king heard thereof, he was wroth and he sent forth his armies, and destroyed those murderers, and burned up their city. (Matthew 22:5-7) That is the inevitable result of your determination that the Kingdom is of sickness and death. Did the king really do that? You bet your boots he did. We'll just bury it under and start over. I don't know whether you want to hear this or not. I'm absolutely not concerned about your denial in aggregate of what I'm offering you. We're going to plow you under and seed again. What I'm offering you individually is the growth of your own association with yourself. You can now see yourself as coming into a field where you are a sport, or separate, in that association. Now what are we going to do? The guys that we thought were going to get it, don't get it. All the plans that we made for the establishment, the Pope, Satchitananda, Buddha, all of the great kings, none of them heard it. What they ended up doing was building temples that attacked God. The rest of the people just went back to fishing. What a strange place to be.

Then saith he to his servants, The wedding is ready, but they which were bidden were not worthy. Go ye therefore into the highways, and as many as ye shall find, bid to the marriage. (Matthew 22:8-9) I want you to understand this. This is precisely and exactly what I just offered you. I am offering you, because of the failure of the establishment —the hell with the agriculture, the hell with the traders, the hell with the temple —come on out and listen to the simple story. The other one failed. Look around you. It's been buried. The Christ has been buried and there is no hope at all. This is your bidding to come to this. Notice I'm not now at all concerned about your qualifications. I didn't actually reduce the step, I took another step. Since you thought qualifications were necessary, you have taken them and made them the qualifications of death. I'm telling you the hell with the qualifications, I'm inviting you as the worst sinner in the world. I don't care if you are good or evil or what your prognostications are, come on in and enjoy this lovely wedding. I'm not concerned about your entitlement to it. I'm giving you the fact of the matter of my whole mind. You are perfect as God created you. Come and enjoy the feast. There are no qualifications! This gets sneaked in because the world is busy worshipping idols or harvesting their own crap. All of a sudden this call goes out with a totality of meaning that transcends the world. And you heard it in your own mind, and now you are going to enjoy the feast of eternal life. And you say to me: what about my concepts? Include them in! ... go ye therefore into the highways and byways and as many as ye shall find bid to the marriage.

So those servants went out into the highways, and gathered together all as many as they found, both bad and good, and the wedding was furnished with guests. (Matthew 22:10) Guys, you listen to me, I'm giving you the fact of the matter: This is a wedding with God. I'm not concerned about your qualifications because the mere idea that you are here is proof of your willingness to come home with me. What are you going to have to do? Be innocent of your old associations. I would strongly recommend, since you are in the presence of the power of the mind of God, that you be innocent of bringing in your intent to justify the establishment or the agriculture or exchange that is going on out there. Come here for no reason and enjoy yourself. You're here aren't you? Be grateful that you found it and that the invitation has been extended to you! Don't try to keep clothing yourself in the guilt of your own identity. Why? I better not read the next sentence. You won't want to hear this. I'm telling you, if you've come this far, you better clean up your determination to come to God. Many of you who have left, for whatever reason, were not willing to totally relinquish the necessity for your own defense of your own existence. This, obviously, is bypassing establishment.

And when the king came in to see the guests, he saw there a man which had not on a wedding garment. (Matthew 22:11) Whenever I look at some of you guys, I say: What the hell are you doing here? You're here, obviously, but the manner in which you are defining your association has nothing to do with what I am offering you. What the hell are you doing here? You are just determined to bring your own self in, and then go out and do some more stuff. How willing are you to be stripped of the garment of sickness and death and guilt that you bring to this association? You have an invitation from God to come to God. It doesn't have anything to do with what you brought in here. Nothing. You are in a place where that can occur! And you say: what do I have to do? At the very minimum I have to wear a fig leaf. Chew on that one. That's just another parable. How come you're covering your privates? You're guilty. This is Genesis –it's the same idea. You came in naked; you go out naked. If you put on a fig leaf, you'll begin to design different kinds of fig leaves. You'll have to compare your fig leaf. Obviously, you've covered your own genetic memory. That's the whole body condition.

And he saith unto him, Friend, how camest thou in hither not having a wedding garment? And he was speechless. (Matthew 22:12) He is thinking, "What the hell are you talking about? You told me to come, I came just the way you told me to." He was speechless. There was no way he could correlate it in his mind the meaning of this. Then he would obviously begin to defend himself.

Then said the king to the servants, Bind him hand and foot, and take him away, and cast him into outer darkness, there shall be weeping and gnashing of teeth. For many are called, but few are chosen. (Matthew 22:13-14) What is the choice of you based on? Your admission of your wholeness. All of the parables will often address the fundamental mistake that was made in our not recovering you initially. *The seed fell on barren land; the birds ate a lot of it.* (Mark 4:3) You didn't have enough water. We understand perfectly that the tares are growing with the fruit. We don't care. We are at fault for the tares growing with the fruit. (Matthew 13:24) But we'll sort that out for you if you'll let us. Obviously the tares are your perceptual associations with yourself, rather than the purity of you. Now I am doing another parable. How else can I explain to you that you are the conflict?

People who are utilizing the power of their minds to bring about healing believe that I am teaching that healing comes about by blind faith. I'm not. There isn't any such thing as healing by blind faith –not in the sense that the association is not healed, but that it could not remain blind as to the method by which the healing occurred. It would require a reason for it. The solution to that has to be that healing is reasonable. I take nothing from the physician except my fundamental declaration to him that existent association is what the disease is. If that will appear reasonable to him, his progress in his own healing will be very rapid, because the manner in which he applies the remedy will be based on a broader range of remedial possibilities. Quite literally, the whole miracle teaching is nothing but the cause and the effect are not apart, and that any remedy will heal perfectly if it is allowed to. It's the admission that the disease is the separation, or the human condition. This is all Mary Baker says. I'm not taking away the premise that the idea of cause and effect relationships can bring about a result. Good grief, that's what you do as a doctor. That's what you do as a human being. You look at the problem, and you solve it in that association. If you want to look at what the Kingdom is, you cannot avoid the idea that the Kingdom of Heaven is based on the premise of your own mind and the outcome you want in the inclusiveness of your existence with the universe. The Kingdom is the result of premises, just as this world is. I'm telling you that you are getting the result of your own mind. I'm adding to that: There is nothing outside of your mind. That's where the conflict lies.

And when the sabbath was past, Mary Magdalene, and Mary the mother of James, and Salome, had bought sweet spices, that they might come and anoint him. And very early in the morning the first day of the week, they came unto the sepulchre at the rising of the sun. And they said among themselves, Who shall roll us away the stone from the door of the sepulchre? And when they looked, they saw that the stone was rolled away: for it was very great. And entering into the sepulchre, they saw a young man sitting on the right side, clothed in a long white garment; and they were affrighted. And he saith unto them, Be not affrighted: Ye seek Jesus of Nazareth, which was crucified: he is risen; he is not here: behold the place where they laid him. But go your way, tell his disciples and Peter that he goeth before you into Galilee: there shall ye see him, as he said unto you. (Mark 16. 1-7)

Be not afraid:
go tell my brethren that they go into Galilee,
and there shall they see me.
All power is given unto ye in heaven and in earth.
Go ye therefore, and teach all nations,
baptizing them in the name of the Father,
and of the Son, and of the Holy Ghost:
Teaching them to observe all things
whatsoever I have commanded you:
and, lo, I am with you always,
even unto the end of the world. Amen.

CHAPTER NINE

Gethsemane To Galilee

I am going to play the part of a savior just for a moment. Am I playing a part? Sure. That is exactly what I am doing. How am I doing? Obviously I have appeared in the world, and I immediately begin to do what? Demonstrate my own experience. I could not *not* do it because it is a part of being in the world. It is the experience of baptism, transfiguration, illumination, recognition of associations that transcended my apparent appearance – but in any regard, I have undergone the entirety of the experience in my own mind and am a savior of the world. What I would attempt to do at that point, just as Jesus Christ of Nazareth will attempt to do, is to show you the totality of our relationship with each other, not based on this world, except in the transcendence of it.

The problem always will be that I must show you an association of apparent death with life. I must somehow demonstrate to you that where you are engendered in the location of your association is not an acknowledgment of life, but an acknowledgment of death. This may appear to affront you momentarily, but if you will look at it in consort with my mind, you can see immediately that people really gather to die. They don't gather to live. Imagine the facility that is made available to them through the human condition – to gather in a dead place, or to gather for that space in time and cultivate it, grow food, live there, associate with each other, in what? A moment of death! Obviously we are gathering where? At the point of death! *And it came to pass, as they were much perplexed thereabout, behold, two men stood by them in shining garments: And as they were afraid, and bowed down their faces to the earth, they said unto them, Why seek ye the living among the dead? He is not here, but is risen* (Luke 24. 4-6) Otherwise we wouldn't know about death. The human condition is not knowing about Life; it is knowing about death. Can you see that? All of us here are aware that we are going to die, so we are sharing that moment of life and death. Right now the human condition inevitably acknowledges that he is in a space/time where he aggregates to live in time and then die.

The principle of salvation says: Since you are aware of a time-and-space association, you must be aware of an alternative to it or why would you bother to die? That is, where do you affront your own condition? Why have time at all? Do you see? There must apparently be, somewhere within that aggregation of separate minds, a single association that will lead you to the truth, first of you, individually, and then in consort with the reality of our mutual grace through the power of love and God.

I am appearing in body for just a moment. That is an amazing idea. We are appearing in body for just a moment.

This is a digression, but I want to read the first page of our Miracles Healing Center brochure. We are teaching healing. Have you heard of the Miracles Healing Center? The astonishing thing about it is your willingness to teach spontaneity of healing. There is not a lot of conceptual association in here. This is very valuable to you. The reason that it is going to be valuable is: you are a healer. Do you see that? This is pure Jesus Christ. Obviously Jesus Christ of Nazareth demonstrated His capacity to change the apparent associations of body. He absolutely did that. He did that before His apparent crucifixion and resurrection. He evolved a capacity of a talent to repair in the entirety of His association with Himself; to bring about a spontaneous reoccurrence of the moment of separation from God to the truth of God.

This says: Miracles Healing Center. When you open it up, it doesn't fool around with the idea that somehow you have to examine your relationship with yourself. What it says is that spontaneous healing is perfectly natural; that there isn't anything wrong with it. The top of the first page says: *The power of mind to heal is a continually-demonstrated fact of life!* See how nice that is? Don't give us that junk about you can't be well. You are demonstrating it continually. You are exercising your power to find a remedy for your situation, and to whatever degree, you are successful about it. Do you see that? So when they say, "What do you do?" You say, "We afford spontaneous healing through the power of your mind." What is your next question? "How do you do that?" You say, "What do you mean, 'how do we do that?' We do it by using the power of your mind to determine the outcome you want in your relationship with yourself." "Oh, I see." What's your next question? "Prove it to me." And you say, "I am!" That's not the question. The question is whether you accept it or not.

I've been at this a long time! And I'm always surprised when it works. Can you hear that? You are always surprised when it works. In your mind, you know perfectly well how it works. The problem is not that, the problem is how can you present it. Amazingly enough, many of you are in that place/time with me now. That is nothing but a place/time of the sharing of the resurrection of our mind from death to Life.

I just want to read you this: *There has been enough speculation, examination and interpretation of the increasing event of sudden very rapid unexplainable healing of bodily disease that is occurring in this world. Many have been unable or unwilling to accept the inescapable evidence of so-called miracle healings and spontaneous remissions and recoveries that are being demonstrated with increasing frequency. Most want to believe and seek faith to do so, but still lack the confidence in the immediate healing grace available through the power of their own mind. This is the provision a Miracle Healer activates and intensifies. It is time to bring the power of our mind to where our hearts have led us. The healing power of God's love is not a remedial medical possibility. It is a fact of the Universal Mind of God that you are perfect as He created you.* That is the first page of our Healing Center brochure. We are teaching the spontaneity of the occurrence and the immediacy of the availability of it through a physical resurrection of your body.

In order to demonstrate that I'm going to play the part of Jesus here for just a minute and I will read how Jesus attempts to demonstrate it in His so-called journey, in His individual journey from death to Life, from crucifixion to Life. When He first tries to describe it, He will say to the associations, "I am about to undergo a completion of my experience in my return to the certainty of my individual saviorship in regard to God." He presents it to them in a particular way – I am presuming that you see that you have been with me in this association where we have demonstrated healing together. What He actually says to them is, "In a moment you will not see me, and then you will see me again." (John 16:16) It is really interesting because they really don't understand Him. But the best way for Him to describe it is to say, "You won't see me for a moment and then you will see me. There is going to be a subtle distance between when I am apparently not with you, and when I return to you because the place in which you will no longer see me is a place of death, not life." It is so great for you to see how the Biblical reference goes. What it is going to say is, "At the place of the crucifixion, where there is apparent death, I am going to spring to Life and be gone for a moment." John 16 says, "Now you see me, now you don't."

All things that the Father hath are mine: therefore said I, that he shall take of mine, and shall shew it unto you. A little while, and ye shall not see me: and again, a little while, and ye shall see me, because I go to the Father. You are going to see me again because I go to the Father, not because I am here. Have you got that? *Then said some of his disciples among themselves, What is this that he saith unto us, A little while, and ye shall not see me: and again, a little while, and ye shall see me; and Because I go to the Father? They said therefore, What is this that he saith, A little while? we cannot tell what he saith. Now Jesus knew that they were desirous to ask him, and said unto them, Do ye inquire among yourselves of that I said, A little while, and ye shall not see me; and again, a little while, and ye shall see me? Verily, verily, I say unto you, that ye shall weep and lament, but the world shall rejoice: and we shall be sorrowful, but your sorrow shall be turned to joy. A woman when she is in travail hath sorrow, because her hour is come: but as soon as she is delivered of the child, she remembereth no more the anguish, for the joy that a man is born into the world. And ye now therefore have sorrow; but I will see you again, and*

*your heart shall rejoice, and your joy no man taketh from you.
And in that day ye shall ask me nothing. Verily, verily, I say unto
you, Whatsoever ye shall ask the Father in my name, he will give
it you.* (John 16:15-23)

A Course In Miracles is lucidly honest in its descriptions of the
travail that you experience at the moment of your own entering into
space/time. The second accomplishment must occur in His sharing,
in my sharing, with you what we are going to term "the agony of
Gethsemane." A journey that leads to Calvary, a gathering that leads
to Calvary, which is a place of death, has no meaning. We continually
gather in associations that justify our death-ness. And we sort out our
Calvarys/Golgothas – places of death, place of the skull – in many,
many associations that justify the killing of our brother and ourselves.
Jesus says, the entire *Course in Miracles,* and my certainty of my own
resurrection, is based on my admission that somewhere in my Calvary
must be first a Gethsemane.

There has to be somewhere that I can come and compare my
associations of death with the peace and joy I would experience in
the communion with you. This is called a garden. The Garden of
Gethsemane. The question is not that; the question is whether it is a
garden of joy or a garden of agony. Obviously, that garden – Jesus has
this experience – must be an ancillary association with Calvary. It has
to be because it is where you pause for a moment to observe yourself
in your relationship with death. You can read about this if you want
to. This is exactly what He says: *'We are going to gather. Come with
me and gather at Calvary."*

This is what He says: *We have been there before. You know
where that is. You come and sit with me and let me show you that
I am not going to be here a minute, and then I will be here. I used
to talk to you in parables. I used to describe to you what it was
like to be here and how I was going to share my own resurrection
with you. Now I intend to demonstrate it.* (John 16:25-33)

What is going to occur? Tremendous travail, because I am in a
place where death occurs. I am not in a place where I have escaped
from death. I must be in the place where space/time began. I must be
at the cradle of civilization, at the beginning of man, where there was

a recognition of a reassociation out of time. What happens? They all gather there. Obviously the world, at this point, is going to be after Him because He is at the point where He is going to make a declaration of eternal life. The heretofore gatherings of all human associations are to sustain and cultivate the earth – to live within the First Covenant, and to die within that association. Yet you see how obvious it is that you must come there in your own mind. He is also teaching that you are coming there in your own mind because He is going to teach physical resurrection of your body.

He says, "Here we go. Let's all get together." Now he is going to instruct them. He is going to say, "I have taught you to love, I have showed you about healing. I am going to leave you for a moment, and you won't be able to come with me, but I will come back right away." (John 17) My entire teaching is that this is going on right now. I don't know whether you are hearing me. I want to read this to you out of the Text of the Course just to be sure that it is in your association of time with me. This is the parting of the veil, partly, and partly it is the direct admission that everything is going on all the time. Let's try it. *Each day, and every minute in each day, and every instant that each minute holds, you but relive the single instant when the time of terror took the place of love. And so you die each day to live again, until you cross the gap between the past and present, which is not a gap at all. Such is each life; a seeming interval from birth to death and on to life again, a repetition of an instant gone by long ago that cannot be relived. And all of time is but the mad belief that what is over is still here and now.* (Text 26:5)

I will back up to one other association that I don't want you to escape in this regard, and it is that you must suffer the agony of the garden. If you want to call it the last useless journey, that is all right with me. But it is impossible that you did not come to the earth. *And now you stand in terror before what you swore never to look upon. Your eyes look down, remembering your promise to your 'friends."* (Text 19:4) Peter says, "I will never betray you." Jesus says, "Yes you will." "No I won't." "Yes you will." "No I won't." "Yes you will." Three times. You will because you are in an association with death. I am going to demonstrate to you eternal life. Then the question is: "Will you accept me?" If you accept it here at Gethsemane, you will resurrect with me. Can you get that? If you deny it, you will be here, and you will have to observe what? My return. I am going to give you – this is in Jesus' explanation of his resurrection talk with Helen Schucman, the scribe of *The Course* – direct physical evidence that following the resurrection I appeared to you physically so you could actually touch me, regardless of how that is misunderstood. He is showing you the physical resurrection of your body through a continuing demonstration of his own temporal reconfiguration.

In Luke, Jesus tells His disciples directly to handle Him: *And he said unto them, Why are ye troubled? and why do thoughts arise in your hearts? Behold my hands and my feet, that it is I myself: handle me, and see; for a spirit hath not flesh and bones, as ye see me have.* (Luke 24:38-39)

Here is the holy place of resurrection! *All of your "friends," your "protectors" and your "home" will vanish. Nothing that you remember now will you remember. It seems to you the world will utterly abandon you if you but raise your eyes.* (Text 19:4) Jesus suffers the anguish. He asks God for relief from it. (Mark 14:36) In the next sentence He says, "I know you're not going to give it to me. The spirit is strong, but the flesh is weak." (Mark 14:38) If you weren't tempted, you wouldn't be there at all. Can you see that? Who said you were perfect? Obviously you are undergoing that experience where? In your own Gethsemane! But at least you are at Golgotha; at least you are at a point where you can see an alternative to gathering at that moment in space/time in order to verify another death episode. Resurrection is at hand!

The amazing thing is, we say the journey to the Cross is the last useless journey. Obviously, prior to coming to what appears to be physical death, the human condition is nothing at all. Yet at the moment of death he lives! Who can hear that? Can you get that? It doesn't make any difference how long time has lasted in coming to that moment. Yet it is impossible that you identify yourself as a consciousness association without having had the death-Life experience, and are continuing to experience it each moment. The question is not how long it takes you to die, but how long it takes you to die and see there is an alternative. That is what this actually says. It is impossible that you won't come to this life place because in truth your bodily identity is the nothingness of death

No one can look on the fear of God unterrified, unless he has accepted the Atonement... Nor is it possible to look on this too soon. This is a place to which everyone must come. (Text 19:4) You must come to your own Gethsemane. You have absolutely no alternative but to do that.

Here you are at Gethsemane. I want you to see what occurs in Gethsemane. Very simply Jesus says this is the place; it is time for me to resurrect. What happens? The disciples fall asleep.

And they came to a place which was named Gethsemane: and he saith to his disciples, Sit ye here, while I shall pray... And he went forward a little, and fell on the ground, and prayed... And he cometh, and findeth them sleeping, and saith unto Peter, Simon, sleepest thou? couldest not thou watch one hour? Watch ye and pray, lest ye enter into temptation. The spirit truly is ready, but the flesh is weak. And again he went away, and prayed... And when he returned, he found them asleep again... And he cometh the third time, and saith unto them, Sleep on now, and take your rest: It is enough, the hour is come. (Mark 14:32-41)

What He wants you to see in that regard is that this is a dream. They are in dreams of death of the association, and He is offering them a dream of Life. In Mark it says it happens three times. He goes out and prays and he's going to bring them all home, and He comes back and what's happened? You are still asleep. You are still justifying your associations with death. Isn't that astonishing? Not only that, but prior to that, at the last supper, He says you will have the travail of the denial of resurrection. It is impossible that you not have that because this world is the travail of the denial of your own resurrection. Isn't that amazing?

The problem is that all of the phenomenal occurrences must finally involve our gathering together at this time to demonstrate our resurrection rather than our continuing crucifixion of each other. Notice how imperative it is that you see that Calvary, the place of the skull, is exactly where the resurrection, physically in your body, has to occur.

I know this will astonish you, but the entire teachings of Jesus of Nazareth is that you will undergo the entirety of the experience based on the certainty that I offer you my body resurrection. I am saying to you that if you want to do this with me, here is what we will do: I will demonstrate to you my resurrection of body at Golgotha. Heretofore, you have seen it as death rather than life. This is literally true in your own mind. The whole teaching is that I am demonstrating to you your own Christhood.

Surprisingly enough, or not surprisingly, I needed, in a particular sense, another place that is a transfiguration of the Garden. While you may rest in the Garden, it is a pre-resurrection place. So where am I going to tell you to come to meet me? Galilee. I am going to take you back to the entirety of our association. I am saying, "Where I am going, you can't go, but I will meet you in Galilee." (Mark 14:28) Once more, come on, guys. This has absolutely nothing to do with the crucifixion, because the crucifixion – death – is nothing. What I am going to show you is that your actual journey is from Gethsemane to Galilee. Galilee will be our identification out of time with each other. Galilee is where we meet, where I met you, to demonstrate. Now, it is very possible for you to meet me at Gethsemane and say, "I am going to Galilee with you." Can you hear this? Why not? You say, "I am going to resurrect. I am going with you." And I say, "No, you can't." And you say, "I'm going!" Nothing could possibly deny you!

Where would we end up? Post-resurrection. You would simply come back and when I meet you, I would say, "Now let's go into the world and teach this." My presumption is you have seen me after my resurrection. The strange part about the entirety of it is that it is impossible to see me in reality except after my resurrection. If you see me prior to my resurrection, at best you will meet me in Galilee or in Gethsemane and share death with me. Well, that is like you falling asleep. You are going to fall asleep again, and I am going to demonstrate the necessity for my crucifixion, and you can say, "Wow, he was crucified and he's dead." No, no. I appeared to you and showed you that I was alive. Your acceptance of it through faith is the indication of the resurrection of your mind. There's not a lot of necessity to describe where it was. He says, "I will meet you in Galilee. I will meet you at the place of the beginning of it."

Notice He doesn't say Jerusalem. Jerusalem is the resurrection of the entirety of the whole association. That's the Holy City. Where we meet is in Galilee with the certainty of that totality. All roads lead to Jerusalem. So you can formulate your Galilee's anywhere that you want. Do you see that? We can associate in Galilee. But remember, it is based on the resurrection, not the crucifixion.

Is it all going on right now? All: Yes! The actual distance of your communication is from Galilee to Gethsemane. Nothing can happen at Calvary, except the entirety of the occasion. If you pile up bones and die there, that's not going to have any meaning. It is necessary that you resurrect out of that association. It isn't that everybody has not had a Calvary experience. They have. Also, it isn't that everyone has not had at least a Gethsemane experience. They could not *not*. Somewhere they have found the peace of God for moments, if only until the time of their ultimate Calvary – if only at the time of their death. It would be impossible to have the idea of death without having a Gethsemane be right there. The entering into the Garden so you can die gracefully is the sign of a Garden of Agony where you have paid your dues in this world, and you gather, and Jesus will be there at Gethsemane. No, He won't! If He is there at Gethsemane, He will immediately say, "Let's get the hell out of here." He will meet you at the point of death, but never to return to death.

If you look at it in a particular way, the way we teach it is: the moment that you are here must be associated with a Gethsemane rather than a Calvary. It is impossible that it not be because Life has to be where death is. Have you got that? Actually that is nothing but the Garden of Eden that you wandered out from and fell asleep. That's not the question. The question is where do you want to hear it? Where do you want to hear that you were tempted in that moment in the Garden to go out East of Eden and die? But you are going to have to start from Eden. Eden is not the ending; Eden is the beginning. Can you hear that? Eden is a holy place or a Garden, Gethsemane, where you come not to die, but to live; not to be guilty of the association, but to be free to return to God.

It isn't that we are not meeting at death, it is that through your denial of death, I will offer you a moment of resurrection that will immediately put us in Galilee, and as you return, having admitted to

Christ's resurrection, you must join with Him in that. And you will not join with Him at Calvary – I'm sorry guys – that was the last useless journey. It isn't that you didn't have to come there, but you had to admit that you were always there; otherwise, you will just get trapped in more time and more and more time will pass.

Helen says to Jesus, "Did you really resurrect?" He said, "Yes." *My body disappeared because I had no illusion about it. The last one had gone. It was laid in the tomb, but there was nothing left to bury.* That is a very interesting idea. If there is something left to bury, you would still be in Gethsemane. You could not *not* be. No part of you remains at that moment of the transformation of your mind. He is going to say that it is possible for you, if you want to, to occur anywhere you want in any time in the body. You can occur as a resurrected body. This is what this says! You can demonstrate very dramatically that my body is resurrected. I am not sure what good it will do you if you won't enter with your mind into the gathering of our body. I am demonstrating to you an incorruptible body; that is, a body at the Healing Center that undergoes a continuing resurrection. I may then walk around in that body and teach from the certainty of my what? Continuing resurrection! Each moment I am resurrecting out of time to eternity. Whatever this appears to be, including miracle healings, I have no objection to that. Why wouldn't you be able to demonstrate the power of your mind through the resurrection of Jesus as the complete association of your incorruptible body to the realization of your perfection as God created you? Is there any reason why you shouldn't be able to do that? Only your determination to die. Only your determination heretofore to be unable through your fear of that moment to admit the necessity for the entirety of the association of what you think is death, to the certainty that it is actually life. You must come to that moment!

[The body] did not disintegrate because the unreal cannot die. It merely became what it always was. And that is what "rolling the stone away" means. The body disappears, and no longer hides what lies beyond. It merely ceases to interfere with vision. To roll the stone away is to see beyond the tomb, beyond death, and to understand the body's nothingness. What is understood as nothing must disappear. Do you understand?

Now, here is my illuminate mind: This world is nothing and does not exist. Why hasn't it disappeared? I am offering it to you so we can share the disappearance! I am appearing for a moment and sharing the illusion. Now, you like the idea that this is an illusion. I am going to share with you the reality of the illusion in its entirety to demonstrate the illusion of miracle mind. Of course it is an illusion. But it is an illusion in the entirety. The idea that I am some sort of phantom figure, or that Jesus comes and is a "spirit", is nonsense. Jesus Christ of Nazareth is exactly as solid as you are. Can you hear me? He is not more or less than what you are. If you are a body, you are the resurrecting body. Otherwise you will try to change your body in association with dying and that is impossible. Do you understand? What is more illusionary than flesh and bones? Or real, if you will let it be? Do you hear that? We are going to teach you that the body is changing all the time anyway. If anybody ever comes to the Healing Center, we are going to say very simply, "You are healed because your body is always resurrecting anyway." You can get that. Your cells are always changing. Why would you lock it into the illusion of shared death at that point, rather than simply undergo your own resurrection. Obviously there is turmoil involved in it because you are at Calvary – you are at the place in your skull where you have made a decision to die rather than resurrect. Do you hear that?

I declare to you, "your physical resurrection". If you gather all of the engenderings of your memory, you will meet at the place of the skull, which is the middle of your skull. That is where the resurrection or the crucifixion occurs. You play out a pattern of association in the Gethsemane of your own association. That is going on all the time. So we are in the skull here with this – in the mind.

Continuing with his description: *I did assume a human form with human attributes afterwards, to speak to those who were to prove the body's worthlessness to the world.* Are you going to be here for a moment in solid body? Are you going to go out and say: "Jesus is resurrected; I know that because He appeared to me and told me that He was. I am going to appear to you right now and tell you that I am a resurrected body. I will also tell you that since you can see me, you must be in Gethsemane with me. That is, you must have paused sufficiently in your own determination to die, to examine the possibility of an alternative." In that sense, we have gathered in the Garden. The question is not that; the question is whether you are going to go back to sleep again. You say, "No, I will never go back to sleep." Really? What are you doing here? I don't need you swearing to me that you are not going to go back to sleep. Three times you said you wouldn't, and three times you did. And the cock crowed. That is the dawning of another day of death, not life. Sure enough, the cock crows and I am stuck.

Peter is fine. Don't worry about Peter. Look at where you find yourself."I will never deny you." What the hell are you doing then?"Well, I am not going to deny you from now on." Remember, you said "now" you didn't say "then". Notice you didn't defend your denial. Can you hear that? The crucial element is: Stop defending your denial. That will just establish what? The Church! The Christian Church is obviously a denial of the resurrection. It is based on Peter who denied God. Christ offers you the keys to the kingdom. Big deal. What kingdom? Peter stands at the gate and invites you to die in order to get there. That is crap. Look at how determined the association is to die in order to justify his own resurrection. It makes no sense at all. And it doesn't make any sense to you any more.

So we are going to share our resurrected bodies through the example of Jesus Christ of Nazareth. You like that idea? That's fine with me. He is not as much a threat to you as I am. You can pretend that He's not here – you can't pretend that I am not here! If you have, you will be returning from Galilee with me. Are you in Galilee? Come on, you are resurrected, aren't you? Do you see that? There is really no difference in the moment of time, which has to be Gethsemane, and in Galilee, except that moment in time. Jesus calls it a Borderland or a place where you are very certain, or a place where we come together through our own resurrections or through your resurrection of me, or my resurrection of you – my recognition of your resurrection.

I recognize you! Re-cognition is an astonishing thing! What it really says is, the entire teaching is: You know me just as well as I know you. Your resurrection is as much a part of me as mine is of yours. In Gethsemane, Jesus prays to God and says I want them to know that myself is yourself: *That they all may be one; as thou, Father, art in me, and I in thee, that they also may be one in us.* (John 17:21)

We are one self together. Our time is up at last. What has happened? I know that you are hearing me. What we are really saying is that we have a sufficiency in Galilee, that you have come and met with me and have admitted, not through meeting me in Galilee, but coming to Galilee through your own Gethsemane. If you meet me in Galilee, you don't need the experience; you already had it. It means that you shared it with me, which is the entire teaching. Boy oh boy, I love to be heard. I love the idea that you can see that I am offering you a complete anomaly. I gave the talk last week on analogue mind. This is the whole *Course in Miracles*, not from a spiritual vernacular. It says that totally available to you in your Gethsemane – you would have to be there – is an entire resolution, not based on death at all. That would have to be some sort of analogue thinking. It is not a digital association of all the things that brought you there. It is an admission that at that moment there is a complete correlation between what seems to be life here and what life really is. Is that so?

That is *A Course In Miracles*. Its origination and formulation from where it could only be, in Galilee, are attested by both the authorship and the substance material to be not of this world's apparent continuum of existent reality. If I have to come to that place of Calvary with you, I will show you that you can stay in Gethsemane with me, and we can shorten time together. If you don't, you will just keep going through death experiences. You are going to have to stand here for a moment. That moment may seem very long to you, because that is where your threat is. You have been trying to escape from the fear of what? Your own salvation! You are trying to escape at that moment from the fear of the resurrection. And you say, "Jesus, don't do that." And He says, "Yes. For a moment you won't see me, and then you will see me." He is speaking in terms that I have just read you here, of a different continuum entirely in the association with what you think this is. Notice that it is a moment of continuum. But it is absolutely a comparison with Gethsemane and Galilee; not of an association of coming to Gethsemane, which is totally meaningless. A place of death is meaningless.

So we are coming from just out of time, where we have aggregated together through our resurrections, and have come back down to teach in Gethsemane. The invitation goes out to people to come to the Garden. They are coming to the Garden to die! Heretofore, they have denied the resurrection of Jesus. Jesus says that in the Course, doesn't He: "My disciples didn't understand." But now you do. Or are you afraid? Why would you be afraid of your own resurrection? Because that is what you are! And that is what subsequently this world is! The phantom figures that you have brought with you justify your Calvary – your death in that association rather than your life. What an amazing idea. But it would be impossible if you resurrected that they would not have resurrected with you. So you say, "I can't meet you here anymore, but I will meet you at Galilee. At least come and see that I am still alive." That is what we are doing. And that is a miracle! It is the certainty that I am coming from Galilee, from that moment of Galilee – where I was born, where I was raised, where I resurrected – to the entirety of our association.

Where are we finally going to meet? In Jerusalem. We will take all of our separate associations of Galilee and bring them together in the Holy City. Each one of us, then, becomes a whole part of the single mind of that resurrection. Where does it finally come from? Your mind! Obviously it doesn't come from Jesus' mind because you crucified Him. It has to come from your admission of His resurrection through your own. Not in any other way.

A Course In Miracles, Jesus Christ speaking to you, defines itself as an observable anomaly. I am saying to you, "Now you see me; now you don't." You can observe it, but it will be an anomaly. There is no manner in which you can "see me now/see me when you will see me." So the Course is an observable anomaly that represents an entire momentary ancillary continuum of infinite proportions – *an ancillary continuum of infinite proportions.* Do you see that? That is exactly what Jesus says. I am going to offer you a moment of eternity that will extend infinitely. It is a continuum, but it has no proportions. Can you get that? It is quantum, isn't it? Everything is going to be included in that.

The Course is an observable anomaly – you can see the resurrection – that represents an entire momentary ancillary continuum of infinite proportion that is wholly and completely available to each and every apparent constituency of separately conceptualized objective condition of self awareness. In other words, any human being. (Ha, Ha!) Do you understand? If you recognize it, you are gone! Standing next to you, I don't care what you are, is a complete solution to your problem. It has to be. So if you have a problem, you are not gone. If you solved your problem, you sure aren't going to be here very long.

My main thing was to get you to resurrect with me so that I could meet you. Then you could say, "Boy, are you resurrected." And I would say, "You bet! Since I am resurrected, I am teaching there is no such thing as death, and I am having the experience of resurrection." You say, "I would like to have that experience." I say, "Do what I tell you: Don't pay any attention to this world, and you will be resurrected." Do you see? Can you see that no one here really accepts that the fundamental necessity of what Jesus teaches are the requirements for your own individual resurrection of your mind/body? Isn't that amazing? Somehow at least at Gethsemane, if you are there, you have to show a little willingness. Any one of you could come and sit with me in my last travail. I will invite you, and you will immediately – this has already occurred – be with me in Galilee. I am going to meet you later, but it is hard for me to explain that to you. You will see me, and it won't be later. It will be earlier! Do you see? You would have to see me in perfection before you could see me in turmoil. It is exactly the opposite of what you think – it's called the reversal of temporal order. You can't possibly see me here, but earlier, you must have seen each other in perfection. It is the exact reverse. Earlier we must have met in Galilee and come back into this. Your admission of that is exactly what the miracle is. How could we meet here? We can say, "This is the place that we would come to die." But if we come here to die, there would be no reason for our life. What would be the reason for our meeting? None! You must find the reason for our meeting at the point of our death. We must come to this spot:

When you come to the place where the branch in the road is quite apparent, you cannot go ahead. You must go either one way or the other. For now if you go straight ahead... you will go nowhere. The way you came no longer matters. There is no part of the journey that seems more hopeless and futile than standing where the road branches, and not deciding which way to go. (Text 22:4)

You have come to this spot, and undergone an experience. We are sharing the totality of the resurrection of your mind. When you look at new associations, you offer them the power of the resurrection of your mind. Will they recognize you or will they fall asleep again? Well, have they fallen asleep once, twice or is this their third time? At least if it is their third time – after I leave, Peter is going to say, "Well, I did deny Him." He doesn't have to go through another 1000 years of bullshit in order to go through what? Another denial. He got his denials over with! Some of you who came around me had to get your denial over. I have no objection to that. I am here to wake you up. The amazing thing is that after the third time, if you don't wake up, Jesus says, "Well, sleep. If you are not going to come with me, you sleep. After I am gone, the angels will come and say 'meet Him in Galilee. '" That is exactly what He says."I am about to resurrect." He actually says that to His disciples, "Come and stand and watch with me. The time is at hand." It is beautiful. Instead they are all sleeping.

You will notice in Mark that He attempts three times to awaken them. Then he gives them that last shot. He says, "I love you, go sleep some more. Whenever you decide you want it, I am a part of your whole dream." It is impossible that you have not had a Gethsemane experience. You couldn't be here. Most of you are in Galilee. Why? Because most of you have undergone your own physical resurrection. Isn't that so? There is no question that we are not from here. We don't even gather, actually, at the place of the skull. We gather at Gethsemane, coming from Galilee, not from here. We are coming from out of time to here, rather than fighting the battle of here, finding ourselves in association between death and life. We are associating with eternity to a moment of Life, rather than all sorts of moments of death in an attempt to find Life. No matter how much we accumulate at death, at Calvary, nothing was going to happen but another pile of bones, but contained in those bones was the resurrection. Those bones will rise up if you will let them! How long did that take? Three days. A day to get there, a day to be there, and a day to get out. What an amazing idea, that the resurrection occurs in-between cells, and you resurrect out on the third day.

At the very minimum, your journey is not to the Cross. It is not a journey to death. It is from Gethsemane to Galilee, if there is a journey at all. Do you understand me? You are going to have to stand for this moment with all the pain and all the fear and everything that has kept you from seeing God. You don't have to admit to the responsibility, but it sure would help if you would say, "God help me" or "Jesus help me," standing with all the pain in this association, because it is impossible that you do not have the solution or why would you be in pain? If you want to measure that as a travail that you have to pay, go ahead. I am offering you the solution from out of time, by the determination that the resurrection has occurred! What more can I say to you, Christians? Why would you persist in denying it and admitting your denial and then persisting in it, rather than admitting to the necessity for your individual saviorship? The whole teaching of Jesus now will be that the salvation of the world depends on you. Can you teach it? No. Can you experience it? You bet! And through your experience you will teach it! It is impossible for me to have had the experiences that I have had and you are now experiencing without sharing the certainty of my whole mind with you. All I am being is who I am and who you are – not even in the travail of coming from what I thought I was but what I must not be. I am not in that battle at all. I have no battle. I am resurrected! If I am, you are!

If you want to deny it and fall back asleep again, after three denials, I will let you sleep. Most of you never get to the Garden at all. Most of you have been plotting and have already condemned me to death. Can you hear this? You have washed your hands of it, but somewhere, Pilate, you have condemned me to death. Now you pretend you are not in that Garden at all – at least until after I'm gone. Then you can examine the phenomena of the association, make it occult so you don't have to enter into it, and that thought will then hide from you the association. It is an amazing idea.

The Course, Jesus' teaching, is a singular acknowledged pertinence to you, in your mind, and total instructional correspondence that proceeds, comes from, an instantly available temporal consortium. Immediately available to you is your own resurrection, that we have met in Galilee, and we are sharing looking back for a moment at what occurred. That consortium of our minds is instantly available through us, because if you gather for anything real, it would have to be to acknowledge the wholeness of our own mind. What a beautiful consortium! It is still a dream. But what a dream! It is a dream of Life rather than a dream of death. Do you see how individual it is in you?

Don't look for the living among the dead, for goodness sake! Why would you want to stand in your Gethsemane and compare it to your Calvary? If you are going to compare it at all, compare it to Jesus who is sitting right next to you in that Garden, having the agony that justifies His own resurrection. Stop sharing His agony with Him; share the joy of His realization of His own resurrection!

The only agony is trying to teach it here! Is it joyous agony? You bet! Because it comes from the certainty of my mind. Jesus says, "I share this with you for a moment – I share your agony from the certainty of my mind." Any agony I feel is your determination not to hear me. That gives me a moment of agony, but just for a moment, since you are not real to me in your consortium of death in Gethsemane. Remember we are always at Gethsemane. We are always at that Garden. If you share it with Life, you will resurrect; if you share it with death, you will be trapped in that association. Have you got that? *A Course In Miracles* deals with this repeatedly, again and again. *You must come to this place!* You must make the decision at that place whether to join me in the resurrection, or to proceed with all of your other old phantom figures of your mind to some sort of idolship of death. What an amazing solution to the impossible problem of your separation from eternal life.

The surprising thing is, and Jesus tries to point this out, is that if you are living with the crucifiers, you will be that. Somewhere you will derive the gratification of your ability to conquer Life – you think you can conquer death by condemning Jesus to death. It is exactly the opposite of what you think.

The Course is a singular acknowledged pertinence and total instructional correspondence that proceeds from an instantly available temporal consortium that is both a denial of... The consortium denies it. I am coming here from where all of you are, telling you this is not true." Why don't all of us know it?" You do! ... consortium that is both a denial of and simultaneously an alternative to your own conceptually-constructed objective existence. Do you see that? Because in the denial is the complete alternative. Do you understand me? You would have to deny death in order to know you are alive! How many times have you had to read that in the Course? Go read it once more. *There is no death, and we renounce it now in every form.* (Lesson 163) *Swear not to die.* (Text 29:6) The hell with it; I am not going to die! I am in my Gethsemane. I am going to sit here and go through my own resurrection rather than letting myself be nailed up to justify the crucifixion. *He that believeth in me shall never die.* (John 11:26) Not that you are going to die.

Obviously, the dead ones say that Jesus died for our sins. The Live ones say that Jesus Lives for our wholeness! See how simple it is? But see how the uncompromising determination must come from your mind to deny the pain and death that is fostered by your own apparent reality, your own conceptual reality.

Your journey to the Cross – from Gethsemane to Calvary – means nothing. It's from Gethsemane to Galilee. The Christ is with you from the point of the crucifixion, not previous to it. If everything has always led you to death, what would be the sense in it? The alternative must exist in this holy instant of our presence of the transformation of our bodies. Is that so? Where are you in your own body identity with that? I have no idea. But unless you are in Galilee with me, you aren't anywhere. You are just determined to die. It is not that you aren't in Gethsemane, it is just that you are going to let me die because you are afraid to join me in death in order to know that you are alive. I appear to be offering you death. I am telling you that this is useless, but I am not giving you an alternative. In that sense, I am offering you death, because there is no alternative to what I am telling you. I am telling you what I just said: You won't see me, and then you will see me. But as long as you see me here, you will see me in death. If you won't see me for a moment, you will immediately join me because by not seeing me you will not see yourself. Did you get it that time? You got it because I fed you a little love! Anyone can get it if I do that! Why wouldn't you? You are standing right next to me. For a moment you don't see me because you have forgiven me. Now all of a sudden you see me alive!

In the Bible, Jesus finally says, "You will understand this later on." He says, "You're not going to see me for a minute, then you will see me." You don't have any problem; you are seeing me all the time. That's only because you have undergone your own resurrection. If you don't see the Christ, it is simply because you haven't been resurrected in your own mind!

All we are really doing is sharing Life instead of death. You are admitting what? You are alive! You have come alive. You say, "Holy mackerel, I was asleep. I was in Gethsemane, there's no question about that. But I had fallen asleep. You tried to wake me up, but I decided to take another 40 winks." So you have been trapped in that 40-day interval; you are asleep in the 40 days before the ascension, which is the final 40-day period. But it would be nice if you would wake up at least somewhere within that association. You say, "Well, it is just going to take me a lot of time now." That is not true. At any moment you can join in the resurrection! That is the exciting part about it. Finally the exciting part about this message is that it is going on all the time anyway. See how much we have shortened time? Immeasurably! You can't even measure it! In Galilee it is measured as holy instants and accumulation with the certainty of the consortium of our love for each other.

He says, "Feel my hand." Is it solid? You bet! Divinely solid. You say, "Why don't you pass your hand right through him; he's just a phantom." You're a phantom; I'm real! I couldn't possibly pass my hand through you. You are all space anyway. If I demonstrated passing my hand through you, it would be the admission of a matter association. Did you hear that? It would be a correspondence with me.

That was a good Bible lesson. This is the time when you are coming and sharing a purpose in its entirety, and experiencing the excitement of associations who are actually going to come into moments of Gethsemane associations because they find peace and joy in commitments. All gatherings of human beings must be for something. When they gather with the single intent, they will always be more joyous than if they gather with an intent to kill each other. It doesn't mean that the battle is not going to occur, but it will occur at a moment where at least some justice has been established - where some rules have been set to which everybody agrees.

And herein is the end of this sojourn into the nothingness of your apparent separation from Heaven and Eternal Life.

Welcome Home.

www.ingramcontent.com/pod-product-compliance
Lightning Source LLC
Chambersburg PA
CBHW060434090426
42733CB00011B/2267